AMERICA'S
ATONEMENT

Studies in the
Postmodern Theory of Education

Joe L. Kincheloe and Shirley R. Steinberg
General Editors

Vol. 34

Aaron David Gresson III

AMERICA'S ATONEMENT

Racial Pain, Recovery Rhetoric, and the Pedagogy of Healing

PETER LANG
New York • Washington, D.C./Baltimore • Bern
Frankfurt am Main • Berlin • Brussels • Vienna • Oxford

Library of Congress Cataloging-in-Publication Data

Gresson, Aaron David.
America's atonement: racial pain, recovery rhetoric,
and the pedagogy of healing / Aaron David Gresson III.
p. cm. — (Counterpoints; vol. 34)
Includes bibliographical references and index.
1. United States—Race relations—Psychological aspects—Study
and teaching. 2. Racism—United States—Psychological aspects—Study and
teaching. 3. Loss (Psychology)—Study and teaching. I. Title.
II. Series: Counterpoints (New York, N.Y.); vol. 34.
E185.625.G65   305.8'00973—dc21   96-54254
ISBN 0-8204-3145-1
ISSN 1058-1634

Die Deutsche Bibliothek-CIP-Einheitsaufnahme

Gresson, Aaron David:
America's atonement: racial pain, recovery rhetoric,
and the pedagogy of healing / Aaron David Gresson III.
(New York; Washington, D.C./Baltimore; Bern;
Frankfurt am Main; Berlin; Brussels; Vienna; Oxford: Lang.
(Counterpoints; Vol. 34)
ISBN 0-8204-3145-1
NE: GT

Cover design by Lisa Barfield
Cover photo of Vietnam Women's Memorial in Washington, D. C.:
created by Glena Goodacre, 1994.

The paper in this book meets the guidelines for permanence and durability
of the Committee on Production Guidelines for Book Longevity
of the Council of Library Resources.

© 2004 Peter Lang Publishing, Inc., New York
275 Seventh Avenue, 28th Floor, New York, NY 10001
www.peterlangusa.com

Printed in the United States of America

For Ariane, Patricia, and Susan;

also for Robert and Jordan;

and the memories of
my mother, Lucy Lee Hargrove,
and my godfather, Jerry Salters

The man who has tripped between death's legs and then
Recovers himself and breathes again,
Can only laugh or only weep:
He has not the heart to mourn.
CHARLES VILDRAC

When enough men have died, then perhaps there will be redemption,
renewal . . . until then, we mourn.
ANONYMOUS

They thought that they would be able to heal their wounds if they
went against Baghdad.
SADDAM HUSSEIN

CONTENTS

A PERSONAL PREFACE

The Dance of Agency in the Twenty-First Century

USA — God Bless Her . . . We'll Defend Her.
Anonymous 9/11 slogan

What does *agency* mean? What is its relevance for the new century in American society? These questions are at the core of this book. But because the subject matter — race, identity, power, and healing — is not immediately understood in terms of agency, I want to use this preface to introduce both the subject matter and the intention of *America's Atonement*.

Simply put, *agency* is the primal cry *I am somebody!* Look up the term in, say, *Webster's II New College Dictionary*, and you will see that the word comes from the Latin, *agens*, and means "effective," "action," "power." The difference between my simple definition and the more official idea is important: my own, which hints at Jesse Jackson's mantra for black Americans of another generation, represents a recent effort by some in American society to insist that the average person, Everyman, has a voice and a personal motive and agenda. The dictionary term harks back to when one acted on behalf of another in whom power and authority resided.

The difference between these two understandings is critical, as they represent two sides of the human condition in which one is either passive or active, giving or taking, losing or winning. Although life is often depicted as either one or the other, we recognize that a truer, less Manichean view depicts us as moving back and forth between these two circumstances. This is why I refer to *the dance of agency*. But why do I suggest that this dance has some special importance in contemporary America?

I began *America's Atonement* in the mid-1990s shortly after the publication of my *The Recovery of Race in America*. Encouraged by the apparent success of this work—it received both national and international honors—I began where this work left off, arguing that a racial recovery was occurring and that we must closely monitor and manage it lest we return to the racist past. But there was an irony in my thesis: if I were correct, there was a good chance that my own work would become problematic and thus marginalized. This occurred when the publisher, having fired its minority acquisitions editor, decided to let my book go out of print despite its relative success.

The firing of my editor was part of a major debate carried in *The Chronicle of Higher Education*.[1] Although he had claimed racism toward himself and other minorities in publishing who did not follow the party line, the University of Minnesota Press "found no evidence of racial discrimination." I felt both guilty and powerless as a result of these events. I felt guilty because I had unfairly and unfeelingly accused my editor of abandoning me when the publisher had tried to suppress my title's message: *racialism continues in America*. I felt powerless because I could help neither my editor nor myself. Indeed, under new leadership in late 1999, the press dropped my book from its list without explanation or encouragement.

What is the point of this story? By 1999, I had been working on this book for nearly four years. Most of the material was collected and drafts had been rewritten. But I could not finish or release what I had already written. Not even the kind, persistent chiding of my friends and editors, Shirley Steinberg and Joe Kincheloe, or the fact that my publisher repeatedly promised on Amazon.com a forthcoming volume gave me the energy and motivation to finish this work. Even my headlong rush toward a broken contract—anathema to a serious author—could not move me. I was deeply wounded and silenced by the fate of my editor at Minnesota and my award-winning book's short life in print.

My writing and publishing a critique of racial relations in the late twentieth century had been an act of agency. The silencing of my work seemed to me an act of counteragency. Both acts imply power. My act represented a belief that I had come far from the Old South where I rode on the back of the bus; called all whites "sir" and "ma'am"; shined shoes for poor, white sailors outside the segregated USO in Norfolk, Virginia; and dreamed of nothing much at all. I confess that I have sometimes said and written things that I would not have done had it not been for the radical 1960s. Like so many, I had found in that decade a burst of freedom, a new voice.

Whatever its motive, the publisher's actions had the effect of reminding me of where I had come from and where I really stood. Sending my work into out of print status was for me a renewal of the older meaning of agency, for the press effectively acted on the behalf of powerful others who would rather not have such ideas circulating society. (In chapter 2, I present material indicating how certain "blind reviewers" of a textbook that I was commissioned to write attempted to suppress my voice by reducing my work to "white man bashing.") Together, my and my publisher's actions constitute a *dance of agency*.

Recent events, including a resurgence of racial discord at my alma mater and employer, Penn State University, have renewed my sense of agency. The recovery of race I foretold in my *Recovery of Race in America* has become the recovery of racism. The concerns I had when writing *America's Atonement* have come of age. But as some have noted, the swinging back of the pendulum from racial consciousness and conscience to the other side does not mean the same old racism. On the contrary, something decisive has occurred, partly because of the mass media and the global political economy and the resulting global cultural condition.

This is a more complex America we now live in: we are unified but complicatedly so, and our relations both at home and around the world are a *dance of agency*. The dominant television media—CNN, MSNBC, and Fox News—daily play out the nuances of this dance. The written media also reflect this dance. For instance, on December 22, 2001, the [Baltimore] *Afro-American* reported the federal government's filing of a $100 million lawsuit against the Cracker Barrel restaurant chain, under charges of systematic racial discrimination in 175 cities and 30 states. But in the same edition of this paper, we learn that Richard D. Parsons, a black liberal Republican, protégé of former New York governor Nelson Rockefeller, now controls the media conglomerate AOL Time Warner.

The contemporary racial context is indeed complex. This global cultural condition underpins how we Americans seek to fuse power and pragmatism in the twenty-first century. It is symbolized by the triad of George W. Bush/Dick Cheney, Condoleezza Rice, and Colin L. Powell. It does not allow for slogans and declarations of either "the end of racism" or "a renewed runaway racist assault." Rather, we are fed a diet of accommodation and annihilation.

September 11, 2001, and the resulting "war on terrorism" are perhaps the best illustrations of this dance of accommodation and annihilation. There are many "sidebars" to the war on terrorism:

- Muslims as targets of "patriotic anger"
- The national debate about ID cards and privacy
- Mourning antiwar marchers

- The minority presence in the antiwar effort
- Rising unemployment
- Stock market agitation
- Erosion of the national surplus
- Executive encroachment on congressional powers

Whatever we understand and feel regarding the attack on our country and the destruction of human life on September 11, it is clear that some people feel terrorism is essential to relieve perceived wrongs and that others feel that it is never acceptable. Clearly terrorism, while unquestionably extreme and perverse, is the birthright of humans and is not unknown in this country: think of the bombings of abortion clinics, Oklahoma City, and so on. But it is perhaps in the war on terrorism discourse that we can best see the complex unfolding of the Us/Them mentality underpinning racism and so many other forms of human oppressiveness. The actions taken to remove terrorism from the planet have stimulated a series of "dances," such as the simultaneous dropping of bombs and care packages on Afghanistan.

Death and dying may or may not change human nature. I have known people whose sickness and imminent death gave them deeper wisdom, compassion, and serenity. And I have seen—even among these individuals—occasions when the darker side seemed to dominate. Nations are much like individuals in this regard. On September 11, 2001, numerous stories of heroism among the victims, their families, and fellow citizens surfaced. Then there were the scandals: some people received more relief money than others; some received none; some people scammed, trying to get money they didn't deserve; the Red Cross itself came under fire and had to apologize for mishandling funds. Nor did the matter of racism escape all reference during this time. For instance, plans to erect a tribute to the heroism associated with September 11 resulted in the so-called Firefighters' Memorial scandal.

There is a broader significance to this debate over who should be memorialized. In chapters 3 and 4, I elaborate on similar dramas, especially over the Vietnam and Vietnam Women's memorials. Here my point is to note that September 11 exposed not only the positives of our national character but also the negatives. The healing, the reach for a higher plane, is often compromised by past tendencies and conflictive propensities. For instance, consider the so-called psychological warfare in Afghanistan. The Bush administration has been accused of lacking cultural sensitivity because of the "doctored" photo of bin Laden on the leaflets dropped into that country after the bombing. Even the retired general Wesley Clark questioned the thinking and wisdom of this strategy. More recently, President Bush's labeling of three foreign countries as forming an "axis of evil" has led to similar doubts. Former President Jimmy Carter described Bush's "mantra" as "over-simplistic, counter-productive, . . . [an action] that will take years to correct."

These cases hint at the complex role of agency and counter agency regarding racial and related matters of social justice sparked by September 11. What they seem to share is an undercurrent of pain, which I focus on in *America's Atonement*. It is because the pain generated by September 11 fuses so often with the pain traditionally associated with racial and social justice issues that I have completed this work. I have come to believe that my silence—my refusal to complete this book—represents a loss. All is not well and no amount of chanting "United We Stand!" can long conceal the many divisions within, divisions our enemies correctly apprehend, even if they fail to understand how we "dismiss" such differences when under siege.

The slogan opening this preface announces the tension and the challenge taken up in this book. We say God is the "first cause" and "final solution" to matters such as "blessing" our nation, but we recognize the need for personal action. This is agency. This is the human condition. This is the dialectical. This book is a refusal to be silent; it is a celebration of hope based on evidence of the possibility for both personal and social growth, even as we surrender to the reactionary and destructive moments marking one side of the dance of agency.

ACKNOWLEDGMENTS

First, to Shirley Steinberg and Joe Kincheloe, friends, colleagues, and editors: their belief in the worth of my thoughts is both endearing and inspiring. Thanks. I also want to thank Chris Myers for his patience and belief that this book would eventually be written and be worth the wait. I hope it proves worthy. Susan Mason has been a major support during the preparation of this work. Thanks. In addition, I wish to thank Derrick Alridge, Patricia Fortson, James Stewart, Lawrence Young, Debbie Atwater, and Cathy Lyons for their support and friendship during my years in "Happy Valley," a site of much pain and pleasure, immense hunger, and final deliverance. A special thanks to Paul H. for his support in the early phases of the project. Also, to the owner and staff of *D'Joint* in Baltimore—Butch, Joe, John, Joyce, Peggy, and Nancy ("Taz")—for providing a special place for me to make it through the drudge of editing! To my new home campuses, Penn State, Delaware County and Great Valley, I am also grateful for providing support in completing this venture. Finally, I thank my many students who shared their stories and endured mine.

INTRODUCTION

What Is America's Atonement?

Two of the things I believe the Seventies will NOT bring are (a) Black or Brown or Yellow Power schools supported by public tax money but run by various minority groups and (b) massed compulsory busing of children to achieve an artificial racial distribution within a given geographical area.

Speaking both as an educator and as an individual, I've been waiting impatiently for the Seventies to get here. Alongside the Sick Sixties, almost any decade in history would look like Paradise Regained.
— MAX RAFFERTY (1970: XIII)

I first used the expression America's atonement to describe the country's efforts to recover from the deep psychological and spiritual pain associated with the social upheaval and crises of the 1960s. Some people felt pain because we "lost" the Vietnam War. Others felt it because America fought the war, and I recall those men who expressed pain because they had been too young to participate in it. Many also felt pain because of the civil rights and black power movements, the peace and women's movements, the gay rights movement, and so forth.

In the opening quotation, Max Rafferty expresses pain and anger at the prominence of multicultural education through his reference to "Black or Brown or Yellow Power schools." But it is his identification of these precursors of multiculturalism as an evil to be eliminated that constitutes *atonement*. The presence of this "anti-affirmative action" discourse in 1969 also illustrates the early genesis of the political activity later associated with Reaganism and the religious right. Rafferty's self-professed alienation from the social activism of the 1960s also reminds us that something very personal, very subjective, was at stake for millions of

Americans challenged by the radical possibilities of the movements characterizing the 1960s.

Max Rafferty's passionate outpouring serves as a reminder that the pain found in so many recent representations of the social changes of the 1960s did not spring forth from nothing. Still, few would readily relate Rafferty's pain to recent discussions of multiculturalism, affirmative action, political correctness, and white male victims. Nor are we likely to see how the social activism of the 1960s later exposed millions of white youth, particularly those in multicultural learning situations, to a special kind of vulnerability: a forced encounter with minorities' often painful images of whites in relation to themselves and their past and present relations. This vulnerability can be seen in these words written by one white male in my course on minority education in the United States: "Every Monday and Wednesday, I come in here to learn about what an asshole I have been throughout history."

This statement might be read as idiosyncratic, and it might be attributed to the failures of a specific teacher or the flaws of a given student. But the current discussions about affirmative action and multiculturalism (Gresson 1995; Kincheloe and Steinberg 1997) reveal the link between individual expressions of racial pain and the social action of the 1960s and 1970s. My student's response reveals, in part, the pain many whites feel when forced to hear about or confront their racial past and present.

The profound, even pervasive, quality of this dynamic is seen in the discourse surrounding the idea of multiculturalism. This discourse has many features, particularly the outrage at affirmative action and related "preferential privileges." The pain and anger expressed by Max Rafferty in 1970 have grown like a cancer. The "cure" for this "sickness" has been a series of social and political battles. The radical 1960s introduced a degree of shared vulnerability. It was no longer a given that whites were "right" and blacks had to "get back"; women were not automatically relegated to "second-class" status; gays and lesbians achieved a space for the open expression of their humanity and right to "come out of the closet"; and so on. True, blacks, women, gays, and others remained vulnerable to the power of those different from them, but now those previously privileged to assume that their views, values, and positions were "natural," "right," and "just" shared this vulnerability. Sometimes blacks, women, and gays even got public support for their experiences, visions, and demands. It is as a corrective to so-called political correctness that *America's Atonement* has found both political and pedagogical expression.

The changes required to bring about social justice may include revelations that are difficult to integrate with one's reference-group identity or subjective sense of self. The pedagogical significance of the role of the pain associated with this kind of learning is seen in the response to the discourse of multiculturalism. It is especially evident in the challenges to the social reform policies metaphorically identified as "affirmative actionism" (Lynch 1997). In an earlier work, Lynch told whites, "talk about the issues . . . widespread talk can be a potent instrument of change" (Gresson 1995: 1). His words are both illustrative and instructive with respect to atonement as recovery pedagogy.

Atonement as Recovery Pedagogy

The August 13, 1999, issue of the *Centre Daily Times* reprinted an editorial from another Pennsylvania newspaper, the (Greensburg) *Tribune-Review*, which argued:

> The U.S. Department of Education's Office for Civil Rights wants to scuttle the use of the Scholastic Aptitude Test as any appropriate yardstick for college admissions. It's a fact that many blacks and Hispanics score lower on the SATs than whites and Asians. . . .
>
> But far from diversity, the result of killing a test that does what it is designed to do—that being to identify the best and the brightest—will only escalate the perversity of what Pete du Pont, the former governor of Maryland, calls the latest "affront on the ethic of merit". . . .
>
> If implemented, the Department of Education's concept of "diversity" will further codify as a "civil right" the act of discrimination to combat discrimination.

The claim that diversity promotes "reverse discrimination" reflects, I believe, a larger recovery strategy (Gresson 1995). This recovery agenda, moreover, renders especially challenging comments like those by my white male student. Without understanding this strategy's influence on the education of young whites, radical activists inside and outside academia will continue to find their efforts resisted, rejected, and reviled.

It has become increasingly evident that the assault on multiculturalism is partly due to the failure to deal more fully with the emotional underside of identity change implicit in radical pedagogies, although some scholars have recognized the presence of this pain (Weiner 1993; Yeo 1997a). I pay particular attention to this subjective aspect of multicultural education. I recognize the discourse of individualism and ahistoricism so often characteristic of many multiculturalism critics, as valid self-other understandings that may disconnect from multicultural curricular efforts, especially if these are more critical or radical in substance and delivery. A major purpose of *America's Atonement* is the illumination of "whiteness" discourses, in particular, as potential threats to students and others exposed to multiculturalism.

In chapter 2, I examine multiculturalism from its position as a challenge to inherited understandings of whites and nonwhites and their respective places as students, achievers, and "inheritors of the earth." White pain is the organizing metaphor for this discussion. White males especially share this pain. I argue that much of the social, cultural, and political action of the past three decades has been directed at challenging the images of the white male as essentially evil. White men have recognized how the ideology and cultural practices privileging them have had a boomerang effect, resulting in their representation in the popular imagination as all powerful *and* all responsible for society's ills. Because of the vast power white men wield, comparatively, it has been difficult to give much credence to individual white male voices disavowing responsibility for various social oppressions. Subjectively, individual white males are not responsible for the structure of society, yet individually and collectively white males participate in the construction of our racial, sexual structure. This represents a paradox for a democratic society.

In *White Men, Women and Minorities in the Workplace* (1997), Anthony Ipsaro reminds us that white men are as diverse and heterogeneous as women and minorities, and accordingly, they constitute multiple identities and infinite possibilities. A democratic society must recognize and nurture this fact. Still, white society has so effectively constructed the world around notions of white and "other" that most of us routinely accept as real these categories and the effects attributed to them. The "essentializing" of individuals and groups is in error and counterproductive for a democratic program of social change. But how do those who have been pre-eminent "essentializers" of "others" renegotiate their own humanity when this has been "stereotyped" into an "essence"? This renegotiation is what I have elsewhere described as the "recovery project" (1995). Here I refer to it as atonement activity to emphasize its "sacred" dimension. This book reflects on several issues pertinent to this atonement activity.

It will be helpful to set the context for our analysis. In particular, what elements promote atonement activity? Given the preceding discussion, at least three conditions appear to enable recovery work: (1) a collection of reactionary images (2) media saturation of the images, and (3) a current, relevant context for concretizing the recovery ideology.

Reactionary Images

Once, in a classroom exchange, a white female student identified affirmative action on behalf of women and minorities as the basis for the greater number of white male than black female suicides. Since the early 1970s, reactionary images have increasingly dominated the popular representation of race, gender, and class, as illustrated in the behavior of the young white female student defending the image of the besieged and betrayed white male. Her imagination had been so thoroughly dulled with respect to certain social justice matters that she was unable to entertain alternative visions and understandings. Furthermore, by resisting the ideas of women and minorities as victims, she was unwittingly reaffirming the status quo. To be sure, women—including this woman—are not mere pawns; it has been repeatedly shown that such behavior has a conscious, self-interest motive (Blee 1991; Ipsaro 1997). Thus it has become preferable to view such incidents in terms of hegemonic dynamics. Nonetheless, with or without women, privileged white men take measures to protect their own interests. Today, according to Anthony Ipsaro, government initiatives on behalf of women and minorities have motivated this self-interested backlash:

> Faced with this confusion and overt onslaught by women and minorities, most White males have gone underground. White men use their present positions of power to defend themselves and covertly subvert women and minorities out of key meetings and informal discussions, and avoid mentoring them. Without this powerful network, many women and minorities fail to move into upper management. If they do move into managerial positions, women and minorities feeling isolated, begin to make poor decisions, and move toward failure. (1997: 2)

Ipsaro reminds us of the obvious: white men as humans are likely to act to protect their interests, right or wrong. Moreover, since society, including the workplace, requires the sharing of information and knowledge for success, isolation or non-inclusion of white males in the diversity discourse leads to minority and female failure in organizations. But to succeed, these efforts to protect their real and symbolic power require the complicity of others. Recent work on white women's roles in the creation and support of "whiteness" (Blee 1991; Fiske 1994; Frankenberg 1993) reminds us that very emotional and relational (parent, child, lover/mate, friend) forces influence the racial, class, and related societal decisions made by white women.

Though various racial and ethnic stereotypes also participate in the reproduction of white male cultural dominance, I forefront one that has ancient roots. I call this stereotype the "pieta embrace" because it recalls

Michelangelo's *Pietà* [Mary and the crucified Christ], sculptured around 1500 C.E. The pose—a grieving female holding a fallen white male—is well known. As I argue in chapter 3, the Pieta Embrace is a central feature of the Women's Vietnam Memorial, marking the reactionary sociopolitical climate of the 1980s. The media's role in promoting a particular understanding of the memorial points to its larger participation in the atonement process.

Media Saturation

Few have to be reminded of the media's strong influence on our culture: from the traditional conversations regarding media and violence (Fiske 1994) to recent self-examination by the media in the wake of the year-long coverage of President Bill Clinton and Monica Lewinsky. John Fiske reminds us, for example, how the media figured in the widely viewed O. J. Simpson trial and Rodney King beating:

> The media do not just report and circulate knowledge; they are involved in its production. *Time* and *Newsweek* were actively involved in producing a particular truth of O.J. by using his mug shot for their covers, and *Time*'s blackening italicized it: the computer enhancement inclined the truth in the direction of white racism. In the same way, the computer enhancement of the video of Rodney King's beating was used by the defense to tilt its "truth" in the same direction. The *National Enquirer* published a computer-produced "photograph" of O.J. in the Bronco pointing a gun at his head and speaking into his car phone, an image that only a computer could produce, for no camera could have been present to take it. Yet this was not a "lie," but a mediatruth. (1994: xxiii)

The media "mediates" messages and meanings. The ways in which white males are represented and understood by the public at large are greatly influenced by the media. A society committed to "atoning" for highlighting white male privilege through various affirmative actions must find ways of balancing the tensions thus created. This is achievable only with the assistance of media that are prepared to favor certain ideologies that aid this process. As the "embedded media" in the Iraqi war illustrate, certain kinds of information receive greater representation: that which legitimizes the presumed imminent war. The vitally critical racial underside of this recovery is seen even with respect to the war: just minutes ago I watched a human interest segment on television, focusing on the only African American fighter pilot—in 2003 nonetheless—stationed at a Virginia air force base. The reporter promises to keep the audience abreast of the airman and his family during the ensuing conflict. Saturation of newspapers, radio and television with certain images is the second element promoting atonement. A third is the climate in which such media flourish.

A Recovery Climate/Context

The 1960s were notably characterized by agitation among various subgroups seeking greater equality: blacks, women, students, the elderly, gays and lesbians, and so forth. The mobilization for liberation, moreover, was simultaneous and often connected with disagreement with U.S. foreign policy in Vietnam and other parts of the world. Symbolically, at least, one prominent object of this social upheaval was the white male. Indeed, much of the recent attention to the "white male as victim" is a result of decades of ideological and rhetoric accusation blaming white males for oppressing everyone else. Before the Iranian crisis in 1979, moreover, black political activism (the 1968 Olympics, Vietnam, Black Panthers, Black Muslims), feminism activism ("bra burning," creation of NOW, and MS magazine), and middle-class youth rebellion (student antiwar movement, hippie counterculture) had succeeded in establishing a cultural alternative to the era's dominant cultural pronouncements. The eventual loss of Vietnam, the return of American soldiers unheralded, and Watergate joined these other forces to suggest a dual and deadly belief: neither American foreign policy nor the American soldier was inviolate.

But the 1990s brought us face to face with a changed vision. It could be seen on the Internet, where James Novak, for example, wrote "Why white men are voting Republican: It's about far more than the economy" (1995, *www.backlash.com/votemale/novak.html*). In a feature, Backlash, put out by Shameless Men Press, Novak argued: "White men will be joined by many minority men because the issues that have made white men angry are the same issues that affect minority men in a similar if not the same way." This piece goes on to identify more than seventy infractions against men—things that presumably enrage all men—but then we get to

65. Men resent that women and minorities are "affirmative actioned" into jobs, promotions, and graduate and professional school openings even when they are less competent than white men who are applying for the same positions.
66. Men resent that those same classes are often excused for their failure to perform adequately in their new "affirmative actioned" positions.
67. Men further resent the same classes above calling white males "racists," "sexist," or some other kind of "ists" for pointing out that white men are smart enough to recognize that a person without adequate skills or experience has failed.

Above, Novak conflates diverse groupings of males into a single category "men." But the insinuation that all men share the same resentment toward "women and minorities" fails to persuade. Perhaps Novak too feels this, for he concludes, in an ironic deletion of minority men,

> White males are angered by indiscriminate and subjective judgments not based on identifiable rules but the whim of the female players. White males are expressing their anger, and expressing it in a socially acceptable way. They overwhelmingly voted for traditional and mostly white male Republicans in 1994. I expect that they will vote in even higher percentages for traditional white male Republicans in 1996. If my predictions are even close to correct, Ellen Goodman and lots of strident feminists should be feeling "anxiety." But they need not get too anxious. White males wrote and passed every significant piece of civil rights and progressive legislation in America.

The years since 1995 have proved to be more complex than Novak could imagine: the controversial election of 2000 and September 11, 2001, frame a different vision than he could have imagined. Still, in 2002, the Internet carries ironically parallel visions. For instance, one site reports the alleged outrage of a white woman responding to the racial turmoil in Cincinnati, Ohio. Entitled "An Angry White Female," it begins:

> Excuse me for being a "racist," but it seems like there have recently been a large number of racially motivated gang attacks against innocent White folks driving by or walking in the vicinity of black gatherings. Is it just my imagination? Am I tainted by the racist propaganda I read on the Internet? The reason I ask this is because when a black mob attack occurs, other blacks join in or cheer the attackers on (Yeah—get Whitey!). They attack the police when they try to protect the innocent citizen. What am I supposed to think, as a White woman, when I hear of or witness these things? Am I supposed to beat myself and demand more "diversity"? Am I supposed to look at the victim as a sacrificial lamb and justify it because the blacks feel they have been wronged by society?
>
> The most recent mob attack was in Cincinnati, following a "peaceful" protest against the shooting of an allegedly unarmed black man wanted on 14 warrants who ran from police and was fatally shot. The police were probably in the wrong. But the violence started right before the politicians began discussing the issue at a forum. The blacks didn't want this discussed, they wanted to loot and burn stores and attack innocent White people who happened to be in the area. What was strange was that the White-skinned leftists who usually incite such acts were nowhere to be seen. Perhaps they knew White people were going to be pulled from their cars and beaten by groups of black men. Maybe they knew White women were going to be

beaten until blood ran down their faces? Rest assured, these White-skinned leftists are all over the Internet trying to defend such acts. One day, the tables may be turned, and if I have any say, the White-skinned leftists will be the first to answer to the Angry White Female.

From this alternative agency now propounded by many whites, we see that atonement has a dual pedagogical significance: to exonerate and educate. In this sense, healing is already embedded in the expression of "righteous indignation." Chapters 1 through 3 illustrate aspects of this self-healing through the demonization of affirmative action, multiculturalism, and other ideologies and initiatives aimed at redressing an historical oppressiveness. But there are other understandings and expressions of healing. These, too, have a pedagogical message and facilitate an alternative relatedness. In Chapter 5 these alternative visions of healing are examined. Often we don't understand difference as a right to be, a press/pursuit of self-interests, dreams, and aspirations. The fear of being stereotyped—made the same, rigidified into sameness, non-different—underpins much white male pain. This is occurring, however, even as many white males continue to rely on society's invitation to hate and demonize the other, particularly black males, in forging a cherished identity by stereotyping them.

Conclusion

We take for granted in 2003 that "America Stands United!" We accept as commonplace similar mantras since the devastating destruction in New York, Washington, D.C., and Pennsylvania on September 11, 2001. Yet for a moment, there was the fear: would we stand as one? After the bitter, problematic election of 2000, we were recognizably a divided nation on many levels: racial, gender, age, class. Even after we had evidence that no "American" terrorist was responsible and we could look for a real "other," we held our collective breath. We exhaled only when "everybody" agreed: we had been done wrong and we would get even. The "war on terrorism" was created.

Few signs of opposition to the war—the bombing of Afghanistan, the depletion of the surplus, the suspension of some traditional freedoms— were evident. Only one senator—a black woman from California—voted against the war. The traditional war protesters, largely downplayed by the media, were themselves muted in their protest, carrying banners of mourning and support for the thousands of lives lost and devastated by the acts of terrorism.

ONE NATION AMERICA REMEMBERS SEPTEMBER 11, 2001

This title introduces "the leather-bound heirloom edition" of the terrible terrorist attack of 2001. It is a picture-laden account of the minutes, seconds, and hours surrounding this period of American history. In its promotional text, we read: "One of the darkest days in our history also marked a resurgence of America's proud, fierce and indomitable spirit." Forefronting the dual icons—the Statue of Liberty and the three firemen hoisting the American flag amid the rubble of the devastated towers of the World Trade Center—this book is more than a fine example of capitalism at work. It truly is a commemoration of recovery.

It is also not surprising that the four-page flyer ironically depicts only white men: firemen, military men, and political leaders. Throughout this book I have been addressing various facets of *America's Atonement* and the recovery accompanying it. We have arrived. A kind of healing has been under way for some years, and it has reached its tentative end point.

The psychology and pedagogy of healing are imperfect, developing sites for personal and collective growth. The recognition of white pain is pivotal to this growth. We must recognize this pain as real, legitimate, and worthy of soothing. Likewise, we must recognize it to be—like terrorism—a problematic response to identity crisis and nonrecognition. The paradox of healing, like the paradox of white pain, instructs us to seek solutions while resisting a regression to the mean, a surrender to power as denial of human limits, mortality.

In the following chapters I consider several different themes—whiteness, affirmative action, multiculturalism, mourning, and healing. These concepts pertain to the human need and commitment to achieve social justice for everyone in the face of a persisting human resistance to see and accept the human condition as we experience it in day to day struggles for survival and perfection. I begin with a selective overview of the contemporary social context within which racial identity is defined.

·1·

RACIAL PAIN AND POWER IN TWENTY-FIRST-CENTURY AMERICA

White Males and the Masculinity Crisis

We are then able to understand that the vicissitudes of every life, just as emotional disorders, invariably engage our narcissism. And the recovery from injuries to it demands the services of aggression.
GREGORY ROCHLIN (1973: 22)

A large number of well-meaning whites fear that they are closet racists, and this book [The Bell Curve] tells them that they are not. It's going to make them feel better about things they already think, but do not know how to say.
CHARLES MURRAY (CITED IN GIROUX 1995: 342)

Prologue

Five years ago, a student in my multiculturalism course suggested using a segment of the film *Higher Learning* (1994) to induce her peers to see racial equality as both right and necessary for American society. Aware of the complexities of her proposed pedagogical strategy, I suggested that some might not see the film's concluding message from her perspective, that is, a call to a nonracist, multicultural society founded on equality and mutual respect. The Monday following our initial conversation she returned to my office. Showing both amazement and concern, she shared with me how her boyfriend, a white male not majoring in education, "proved" my point: "He watched the movie with me over the weekend. He said the movie made him want to be a white supremacist; he said the message was that whites ought to rule."

His position was surprising to her. But his attitude seems precisely what Robert H. Bork argues in his *Slouching Towards Gomorrah: Modern Liberalism and American Decline*:

> Multiculturalism is a lie, or rather a series of lies: the lie that European-American culture is uniquely oppressive; the lie that culture has been formed to preserve the dominance of heterosexual white males; and the lie that other cultures are equal to the culture of the West. What needs to be said is that no other culture in the history of the World has offered the individual as much freedom, as much opportunity to advance; no other culture has permitted homosexuals, non-whites, and women to play ever-increasing roles in the economy. . . . What needs to be said is that American culture is Eurocentric, and it must remain Eurocentric or collapse into meaninglessness. (1996: 311)

Although these are not the precise words of my student's boyfriend, they convey his understanding of the movie *Higher Learning:* to be a white supremacist is desirable. Bork also reminds us that some important things have been happening in America's literary circles that promote the ordinary citizen's "relearning" of a supremacist attitude. Note that Charles Murray, coauthor of the highly hyped *The Bell Curve* (1995), is cited in the opening epigraph of this chapter in a related context: he's telling white people that it's OK to feel what they feel, that science validates their cognitive and moral superiority over others. In addition, I should note that Herrnstein, Murray, and Bork all enjoyed the patronage of conservative-backed think tanks and publishers.

This confluence of thinking about race matters reminds us that interpretation is a vibrant, even dialectical, process. Meanings are constructed and shaped by human beings. The young woman in the preceding story assumed her boyfriend shared her vision, that his and her identity needs were the same. I have argued that this may not be the case (1995, 1997). While it is not necessary that whites realign with supremacist ideologies, the invitation is being offered to them. Accordingly, many young people have identified several discourses that allow them outlets for their frustration and pain. The confluence of visions between, say, Bork and this young man is aided by a peculiar understanding of multiculturalism: "That multiculturalism is essentially an attack on America, the European-American culture, and the white race, with special emphasis on white males, may be seen from the curriculum it favors" (Bork 1996: 304).

The young man mentioned above understood the "attack" implicit in multiculturalism as such when he responded that *Higher Learning* made him want to be a white supremacist. His attitude seems consonant with Rochlin's assertion that "wounds to the ego" stimulate aggression. We have been watching the emergence, consolidation, and execution of this aggression for the past twenty years in American race relations (Gresson 1995). We have yet to adequately conceptualize the emotional underpinning of this aggression. In this chapter and the next, I revisit the multiculturalism discourse and its related issues—diversity, preferential privilege, racial chauvinism—from a perspective I call "white pain." To clarify its meaning and importance, I begin with a closer examination of racial pain.

Racial Pain: A Perspective

Focusing on whiteness as a subject matter can be tricky. Perhaps Michael W. Apple put it as well as anyone in the foreword to *White Reign:*

> Having Whites focus on whiteness can have contradictory effects, ones of which we need to be well aware. It can enable people to acknowledge differential power and the raced nature of everyone—and this is all to the good. Yet it also can . . . run the risk of lapsing into the possessive individualism that is so powerful in this society. That is, such a process can serve the chilling function of simply saying "but enough about you, let me tell you about me." Unless we are very careful and reflexive, it can still wind up privileging the white, middle-class woman's or man's need for self-display. (1998: xi)

Michael Apple speaks a profound truth: the white person's need for self-display in relation to nonwhite persons is a constructed yet interstitial need. It is constructed by the specific values that Caucasians have evolved over the centuries in relation to other segments of humanity; it is interstitial because the need has been woven into the cultural character (Kovel 1970). Nonetheless, this is a need that few whites readily recognize until they have been denied self-display. Let me be clear: whites do not hold a monopoly on this need; it is rooted in the biology of humans and finds expression in what Sigmund Freud called "primary narcissism." The point here is that race, ethnicity, class, and gender are major organizers for those who believe they are entitled to self-display.

I recall my most moving encounter with this propensity. In 1980, I was on tour in Africa for a month with fifty other Americans—half of them white, half black—from across the United States. This was a special, privileged group of world travelers; still, we were largely average Americans.

All kinds of characters could be found among the fifty. But one thing stood out within a few days: attitudes toward the various encounters we had as we crisscrossed the African continent differed greatly from a racial perspective. The greatest difference was the whites' inability to adjust to being "not special." They had the unique difficulty of being told by black Africans where to go, what to do, and so forth. In addition, perhaps for the first time in their lives, these twenty-five "majority-group members" had to live—eat, sleep, socialize—with twenty-five "minority-group members" in countries dominated largely by people defined as "minority-group members." By the trip's end, most of the whites were noticeably depressed, frustrated, and angry. This trip had been nothing like their little jaunts down to the West Indies or South America, places noted for catering to American tourists. Only recently have I understood that their pain might be given a name, *white pain*. But to understand what I mean by white pain, let me first define racial pain.

Racial pain is pain caused by voluntary or forced identification with a "spoiled racial identity" (Goffman 1963; Gresson 1982). It can be viewed as a felt absence of power and the strong presence of guilt and shame. Many people express racial pain. I am an African American male, and I routinely feel racial pain. The other day a neighbor asked me whether I thought my race might be the reason that a house I have been trying to sell has not yet sold. I felt shame at his articulation of my vulnerability as a black man, for I indeed wondered whether this might be the reason my house has not sold. In fact, a day earlier, a Chinese family hastily went through my home after calling me to see it. As they departed, they remarked, in seeming amazement, "You have certainly kept it clean." I felt horrible for just a few minutes after this encounter. I knew that Asians are not necessarily prejudiced against African Americans; I also knew that this family may have meant nothing "racial" by their comment. Still, given the racial history of the United States and much of the world, their words symbolized more than they perhaps meant. I felt racial pain.

Racial pain is created, not inherited. Paradoxically, it is often created even as one seeks to enlarge or negate "race." For instance, when my daughter was barely four, she asked me whether one of her close friends was white. Although this child was from a biracial family, he did not seem to me to be difficult to identify as "black." Over the next several months my daughter asked me the same question regarding other light-skinned blacks. I soon got the idea that she was in the process of constructing race. Moreover, I saw that I was colluding with her by treating as absolute, factual, or essential something that she correctly failed to see as "self-evident."

The point is that we all can damage the identity formation and freedom of our young. And if we are not careful, this can promote confusion. I first noticed this confusion while conducting a psychological study of black female identity issues. In my book partly based on this study (1995), I presented the case of Eartha, a black woman conflicted about her value and worth as a black woman. Rejecting her inherited vision of reality, including racial reality, she tried to construct a privatized understanding of it. But she was unable to sustain this vision when her white friends relied on past ideologies to understand her and her behavior. Nor could she escape her gender labeling and her "matriarchal heritage." When I asked whether she thought being a black woman had been helpful to her, knowing that she had earlier disclaimed the meaningfulness of the label, she replied as follows:

> Yes, it has. It's helped me because black females don't have that many . . . people don't have too many expectations of where they are coming from or how they are. A black female is real hard for people to put in a . . . to define. There is an expectation but there really isn't. People don't really know what that expectation is.

Eartha was closing in on a generally under-examined idea: society's relative ignorance of black women because of the few dominant expectations and stereotypes of them. She continued:

> Yeah, we don't know what to expect. I myself don't know what to expect from some black women! . . . I just don't know what to expect of people because I look at people. I don't know what to expect from a black man, I don't know what to expect from a white man, I don't have that all laid out. I don't write scripts before I meet people to play through or run successfully. And I think a lot of the problems that we put ourselves in is that we write scripts even before we meet somebody. A lot of this is us, it's us. We are writing our own scripts—we are fantasizing—what we expect or how we expect one to respond to us. And the only way you can expect one to respond to you is to truly know how you are projecting yourself. To truly know yourself is to have an idea of what to expect, and it goes across the line with anyone. And a lot of people don't understand the chemistry we give off to a lot of people.

Asante (1988) correctly saw racism as a core contradiction in American society that influences much of black identity development. Caught in her own contradictions, which were tied to the larger societal contradiction, Eartha grappled with her mother's fears and her friend's caution regarding intimacy with a white male:

I don't want to be any color. I want to be me. I am me. I am a female. I realize I have brown skin. I enjoy having brown skin. I am thankful to have this color when we talk about visual effects. I like my color, you know. I am proud of it. Artistically speaking, if I had a choice, I would keep this color because I think it is much more attractive. But that doesn't have anything to do with race.

Freed of collective context and support, such words become problematic. I asked Eartha to explain what her color pertained to if not race.

Uh, my color? . . . I'm proud . . . I don't know how to explain it because I don't put things in a category. I can confuse myself when I try to understand it . . . how I look at it . . . I don't want to put labels on anything. I don't want to be labeled as a female, as a black person. I want to be labeled as an earthling. Maybe I want to go to another planet. I've had it with this planet; I mean it!

Many blacks struggle to renegotiate their space in a white- and male-focused world. How they go about this negotiation is not always easy to understand. In Eartha's case, the contradiction, her own sense of confusion (she can acknowledge it but can find no source for it), is balanced and sustained by the ideology of the black male's fear of black women. She defines herself as a strong but "ambiguous black woman." She disavows the force of race except as an aesthetic quality.

Yet the racial pain Eartha felt is not wholly unique to blacks or any other racial or ethnic group. We all can feel hurt when we are treated unfairly or badly because of our group identification. Pain becomes racial pain through the linking, grafting, or fusing of the psychophysical to specific "racial" identities and socially meaningful occasions. Racial pain as defined here has many nuances or dimensions. One feature with which I am concerned is vulnerability, which I consider crucial to the experience and expression of pain and recovery. Let me illustrate using the case of white and black parents of biracial children.

A white father with biracial children refuses to acknowledge their racial history. Because they are growing up in a privileged, tolerant, white environment, he insists that race does not touch them. He rants and raves because his daughter's skin and features are not given greater positive social assessment because of his whiteness. Then, when she goes off to college, she has an identity crisis, based partly on the difficulty she has negotiating a white or mixed racial identity. A black father reveals a similar refusal: when his biracial son is unable to woo white females in his upper-middle-class New England town, the father grieves, finding exoneration only when his son "wins" an Asian American girlfriend.

Of course, other parents can "acknowledge difference" (Kirk 1964) without becoming bitter or alienated. The point is that racial pain is possible because most humans identify with racial categorization, internalizing many of society's valuations—positive and negative—of the traits attributed to different racial groups. Thus we must be clear about the significance of the contemporary debate and discussion about race matters in the academy. Moreover, we need to be alert to the strong emotion underpinning the logic of disavowal. Racial pain must be considered because otherwise one's penned-up racial energy may burst forth. As research has indicated, culture also largely dictates who will most likely express racial rage through out-group violence (Breen 1965; Slotkin 1973). Thus it is especially important to reckon with white pain.

White Pain: A Peculiar Racial Pain

White pain is a form of racial pain. Because racial pain is typically related to the underdog, who has less social power, we often miss its presence among more privileged racial groups in the United States. But it's real. White pain is linked to a "white identity." Both terms allude to another idea: "whiteness." Whiteness—much like "maleness"—is a complex idea. I use the term to describe feelings that many whites report as a result of others' views of them. This is particularly true for privileged white men. (It is virtually impossible to talk about white pain as an identity marker without shifting to the white male, a shift that indicates the centrality of white men to any discourse in our Eurocentric society. This point is taken up in a later section.) For instance, Anthony Ipsaro writes in *White Men, Women & Minorities in the Changing Work Force* the following:

> Women comprise the majority of the United States population and nearly half of the U.S. labor force. Immigrants and other minorities are expected to constitute a fifth of the labor force in another ten years. Today's interpretation of our founding documents promise equal access to the resources and wealth of this country. Yet White males continue to dominate leadership positions in America, in the corporate workplace, military, government, schools, churches, and the media. Women and minorities are asking, "Is this fair?" And White males are squirming. Their anxiety comes not because White men think they are the bad guys, but because others are treating them as though they are the bad guys: their partners, their children, women and minority co-workers, and younger men. (1997: 1)

Talk about white male pain is not new. At several important points in this country's history, white males have felt under siege or abandoned because of their race (Roediger 1991). Notably, in the past, less privileged white males were called on to relinquish part of their racial privilege in order to include minorities, especially black males, in their unions and other labor-related fraternities and markets. Today, according to Ipsaro, the role of government initiatives on behalf of women and minorities appears especially troublesome; this affirmative action is "confusing" for white men.

White male "confusion," Ipsaro believes, is due to their observing "women and minorities wave the equal opportunity banner and use gender, color, and difference to gain monetary advantages and power positions. He watches these same women and minorities support cultural institutions (e.g. churches) and societal norms (the man as protector) that practice discrimination and oppression. This is confusing" (1997: 2). It is the pain generated by "confusion," contradiction—in himself as well as others—that may partially blind the white male to the continuing racial, gender, and class disparities and injustices in this country. Two other forces are operating as pedagogical cues in shaping this pain into specific discourses and convictions: (1) the role of the media and other societal institutions in promoting specific representations of white males versus the "other" and (2) personal biographies of "nonreciprocated" compassion.

During the past several decades, many thousands of white males have become victims of economic recession. As thousands of blue-collar jobs and many middle-level, white-collar positions have been eliminated, these men have awakened to the realities racial minorities have long endured: a shrinking space for personal growth and advancement. One effect of this trend has been the decrease in the number of white males enrolling in and completing college. As a consequence, some white males are feeling the loss of privileges traditionally available to them. Simultaneously, they were once bombarded with media images and liberation conversations in which they were identified as the oppressors of African Americans, women, and others. It is in such a context that we must understand and address the widespread malaise attributed to many white males, both on university campuses and at various sites celebrating white supremacy. For too many of these men, the past and its relation to the present are unclear, and they respond with a "disavowal of deviance" or reject being identified with the representation of white males as oppressors. Instead, they offer a discourse of white male victimhood.

The perception of a new, invidious oppression of white males has led to some fascinating judicial results. Besides the landmark cases reversing affirmative action in California and Texas, the courts have affirmed the presence of unfairness to whites. For instance, in the *Chronicle of Higher Education*, Katherine S. Mangan wrote:

> Three white law professors who claimed they were discriminated against by administrators at the historically black Texas Southern University have won a round in court. A federal jury awarded $169,000 in back pay and damages to the professors, Eugene Harrington, Thomas Kleven, and Martin Levy. The professors apparently received about $4000 less than their black colleagues with comparable experience. . . . The university is expected to appeal. "This is obviously a time when white males feel threatened, and it's something that African Americans are going to have to deal with," Mr. Douglas [a school official] said. (February 3, 1995: A18)

This is a powerful statement: white males feel threatened. When we refuse to hear and respond to this in a conscious, forthright manner, we invite disaster. Some people, I am sure, would argue that the homeostatic principle will correct things, that the pendulum will swing back to the right and correct for errors of the left. This type of thinking is faulty for many reasons I cannot take up here (Goldberg 1994). What is of immediate importance is that we recognize the psychic assault that multiculturalism—as fact and fantasy—has "inflicted" on whites.

The evidence for this statement is perhaps best seen in the discourse regarding the young, working, middle-class white male student. Various early discussions of white male victimhood as a result of affirmative action policies by courts and bureaucrats have coalesced as the metaphor of the alienated white male.

White Pain and the Alienated White Male

What is alienation? Alienation has been given a variety of definitions, mostly by sociologists. It has come to be defined as helplessness, uneasiness, normlessness, and meaninglessness (see Gresson 1982). Thus it is perhaps understandable that many would say that alienation is a feeling of strangeness with something—person, place, or thing—with which one ought to be "at home." For whites, notably white men, it may be clear how multiculturalism and affirmative action of any sort might bring them to the threshold of alienation. In 1989, Frederick R. Lynch, a sociologist, reported the results of his survey of white males. Entitling his study *Invisible Victims: White Males and the Crisis of Affirmative Action*, Lynch provides one of the most comprehensive discussions to date of what I call white pain.

> "What can we do?" sighed a nervous Midwestern Democratic party official when asked about Stanley Greenberg's findings of anti-quota feelings among whites. "White males between the ages of twenty-eight and forty seem to think they're locked out. What are we going to do?"

Such remarks capture the relational character of white pain. They also reflect the powerful role social critics, including scholars like Lynch, assume in the construction of the discourse against affirmative action. Identifying affirmative action as the villain, scholars like Lynch sometimes go beyond description to prophecy and prescription.

> This drive to reshape American society is colliding with the serious tensions produced by affirmative action. Even more serious conflict many lie ahead. As always, the young are less restrained by tradition and convention. . . . They are less willing to become a new generation of invisible victims.
>   Unfortunately, some anger against affirmative action may have surfaced in the form of ugly expressions of racism. There is racism among the young just as there is among their elders. But sociologists and journalists should not be so quick to label all objections to affirmative action as racist. (Lynch 1989: 177, 181)

It also is clear that the beginning of the new millennium finds Lynch's implied prophecy near fulfillment: everywhere affirmative action gestures have fallen off even as the backlash against "forced diversity and equity" continues against a largely hollow rhetoric of diversity. But to see political conservatism as the basis for this retreat to the right is inadequate. What must be undertaken concurrent with political analysis is "emotion analysis." A few scholars have moved toward doing this. For instance, drawing on the theoretical work of W. E. B. Du Bois, Howard Winant wrote:

> Not only blacks (and other racially-identified minorities), but also whites, now experience a division in their racial identities. On the one hand, whites inherit the legacy of white supremacy, from which they continue to benefit. But on the other hand, they are subject to the moral and political challenges posed to that inheritance by the partial but real successes of the

black movement (and affiliated movements). These movements . . . deeply affected whites as well as blacks, exposing and denouncing often unconscious beliefs in white supremacy, and demanding new and more respectful forms of behavior in relation to nonwhites. . . . Obviously they [the movements] did not destroy the deep structures of white privilege, but they did make counterclaims on behalf of the racially excluded and subordinated. As a result, white identities have been displaced and refigured: they are now contradictory, as well as confused and anxiety ridden, to an unprecedented extent. It is this situation which can be described as white racial dualism. (1997: 41)

"Racial dualism" is not a new experience for whites, even though contemporary times have brought forth its reemergence, perhaps on a larger scale. We need only consider Thomas Jefferson, the gifted American president. Both his personal life—a long term affair with a mulatto slave woman, Sally Hemings—and his famous reflection, *Notes on the State of Virginia* (1781–82), reveal a man torn by conflictive and contradictory identities. He clings to both racist and libertarian value systems. He denies black humanity even as he participates in and co-creates it. And at the end, he left behind both "white" and "black" descendents. This is a personal genealogy, but it is collective as well. The very contradictions and confusions lived out by his progeny further remind us that "white dualism" is a longstanding reality of a racist society. And within this very contradiction, denial and regression continue to compromise the transformative possibilities of the nation. The behavior Winant identifies as dualistic may not be a new phenomenon, created by a rupture in a unified, wholistic, white self-image and identity. Still this behavior does have important relationship to what seems to be a critical contemporary identity crisis among white men. This behavior is too often hastily identified as "backlash," yet as quickly glossed as "inevitable." What is less realized is the psychological or developmental significance of this behavior. Within the recent discussions of "angry white males," we can discern aspects of this psychological challenge and locate some of the important ways it informs emerging race and gender relations.

Manhood and "Angry White Males"

White working-class men represent a position of privilege at the same time they represent the loss of such privilege. It is this simultaneous moment of privilege and loss that we excavate when we turn our attention to the production of white

masculinity. It is their whiteness and maleness which privileges them. But it is also in this space of historical privilege that they begin to confront the realities of loss.
WEIS ET AL. 1997: 210–11)

The class feature of America's atonement may be underexamined in a society committed to denying its class basis. I have not directly announced and unpacked the significance to the "angry white male" metaphor of the intersection of class, race, and gender. I say metaphor because ultimately, class notwithstanding, the term applies to "white man." But scholars and researchers, especially feminists and those concerned with gender studies, have increasingly homed in on the impact of changing material conditions on white male identity. For example, I noted earlier that during the Million Man March, many white males asked black males if they were atoning for their wrongs toward white men. How does one make sense of this? Easily, if we understand that whiteness, particularly white male identity, is largely defined by its relation to others, like women, blacks, new immigrants, and gays.

White pain, the organizing concept of this book, pertains to loss. It signals the loss of the axis around which so much of white identity has been constructed in the United States (Roediger 1991; Slotkin 1973). During the period of slavery, for example, working white men were encouraged to accept slavery as God's will and told that menial work was antithetical to the meaning of being white. And to be male has meant that one is not only unlike the bestial black male (Bederman 1995) but also that being a (white) man is the negation of being a woman (Lyman 1981).

The changing world has gradually chipped away at this sense of self. Even before de-industrialization in the United States, we had evidence of this white male pain. In Europe, after World War I, for instance, men returning from the battlefields found women working in jobs and occupying social spaces once reserved for them. Much of the poetry and writing created during this postwar era reflected their grief, confusion, and anger. The last thirty years or so of American social history have rehearsed precisely this pain, although in different forms and in response to localized intrusions into white male dominion. In particular, scholars such as Stanley Aronowitz, Henry Giroux, Lois Weis, Michelle Fine, Joe Kincheloe and Shirley Steinberg have addressed white male angst and anger in terms of its implications for a diverse democratic project. Gail Bederman concludes in her brilliant study of gender and race between 1880 and 1917:

First, the history of manhood and "civilization" suggests that contemporary difficulties facing poor and working-class men of color in the United States may have a cultural basis, in addition to their widely recognized economic and social basis. Whiteness has long been an intrinsic component of middle-class ideologies of manhood. This may well complicate many men's ability to gain the status of "men" in our patriarchal society. In other words, for men, just as for women, gender can complicate and exacerbate the cultural forces leading to racism.

My major point is simpler, less tentative, and should by now be self-evident. This study suggests that neither sexism nor racism will be rooted out unless both sexism and racism are rooted out together. Male dominance and white supremacy have a strong historical connection. (1995: 239)

Jack Johnson was the first African American world heavyweight boxing champion. I highlight him because his fate, relative anonymity, reminds us what a problematic racial attitude can lead to. Johnson was a "bad actor": he taunted white opponents and chose white female mates whom he sometimes battered. The time was the turn of the twentieth century. The championship fight was fought on July 4, 1910. Johnson knocked out Jim Jeffries, who had retired undefeated six years earlier and returned to regain the title from Johnson, who had won it by knocking out Tommy Burns. Noting the white male effort to assert his primacy during this period, Bederman maintains: "Johnson was equally insistent upon his masculine right to wield a man's power and authority. He treated minor brushes with the law—his many speeding tickets and automobile violations—contemptuously, as mere inconveniences which he was man enough to ignore" (1995: 9). She continues:

As immigrants wrested political control from middle-class men in one city after another, a very real basis of urban middle-class men's manhood received both symbolic and material blows. Immigrant men's efforts to control urban politics were, in a very real sense, contests of manhood—contests which the immigrants frequently won.

Faced with the unthinkable—a black man had been crowned the most powerful man in the world!—interest in pugilism rebounded. The white press clamored for Jeffries to return to the ring. (Bederman 1995: 13)

Bederman explains:

Ever since 1899, when Jeffries first won the heavyweight championship, he had refused to fight any Negro challengers. Jack Johnson first challenged him as early as 1903. Jeffries replied, "When there are no white men left to fight, I will quit the business. . . . I am determined not to take a chance of losing the championship to a Negro." Ever since 1882, when John L. Sullivan had won the title, no white heavyweight champion had fought a black

challenger, even though black and white heavyweights had previously com-
peted freely. (1995: 1)

Jeffries's return to fighting began what came to be called the saga of the
"Great White Hope." But Jeffries's loss resulted in a form of intimidation
that even today we do not adequately address. The destruction of prosper-
ous black communities in Florida and Oklahoma during the early 1900s
are two such examples, and in the recent tragedies in Jasper, Texas, and
New York City, white male violence against black males rehearsed the response to Johnson's victory over Jeffries. According to Bederman,

> The ensuing violence showed what a bitter pill that was for many white
> American men to swallow. Race riots broke out in every Southern state, as
> well as in Illinois, Missouri, New York, Ohio, Pennsylvania, Colorado, and
> the District of Columbia. . . . Even the United States Congress reacted to
> the implicit aspersions Johnson's victory cast on white manhood. . . . Within
> three weeks, a bill suppressing fight films had passed both houses and was
> soon signed into law. (1995: 2–3)

Bederman goes on to argue that the excessive response to Jack
Johnson's victory was due to an important development:

> Between 1890 and 1917, as white middle-class men actively worked to rein-
> force male power, their race became a factor which was crucial to their gen-
> der. . . . During these years, a variety of social and cultural factors encour-
> aged white middle-class men to develop new explanations of why they, as
> men, ought to wield power and authority. In this context, we can see that
> Johnson's championship, as well as his self-consciously flamboyant, sexual
> public persona, was an intolerable—and intentional—challenge to white
> America's widespread beliefs that male power stemmed from white supre-
> macy. Jack Johnson's racial and sexual challenges so upset the ideology of
> middle-class manhood that both the white press and the United States
> government were willing to take extraordinary measures in order to com-
> pletely and utterly annihilate him. (1995: 5)

Today, very few people remember Jackson. Indeed, some histories of
boxing never mention him as the first African American heavyweight. Yet
Jackson, whom Muhammad Ali identified as his "spiritual father," was apparently multilingual and cosmopolitan, an anomaly in his time. Moreover, his insistence on his dominance as a man signaled a crisis for white
manhood because race, along with economics and gender relations, participated in the construction of white manhood. The point? Saving face,
an idea we like to restrict to the Asian patriarchy, is very much a part of

American manhood dynamics (Horrocks 1994, 1995). There is considerable evidence that white pain is viscerally linked to white male identity as subjective experience and socially constructed ideology (Ipsaro 1997). The panic I speak of is broader than white males; black and other racial/ethnic males signal a shared fear with respect to the identity possibilities and challenges emergent from gender dialectics. But white male identity issues eclipse the others for the very fact that white male identity is constructed against not only gender and class but also racial categories. This is seen, for instance, in the recent upsurge of public discourse around blackface on the college campus. The resurgence of this persistent racial "mytheme" is very instructive on the connection between white pain and male identity.

Blackface and Racial Pain

Just months after 9/11, when the country was "united," a scandal hit the presses: "Frats suspended for racially offensive costumes" (*new.blackvoices.com*, November 13, 2001). The Associated Press reported:

> Auburn officials said two students were expelled from Delta Sigma Phi, which along with Beta Theta Pi held a Halloween party in which some members dressed up in Ku Klux Klan robes and Blackface, including one with a noose around his neck. . . . In another photo, fraternity members are wearing Blackface, wigs and shirts with the letters of Omega Psi Phi, one of four predominately Black fraternities at Auburn. . . . None of the students have been publicly identified.

On the previous day, Monday, November 12, 2001, in a piece entitled "Auburn Frat Boys Dumped for Race Incident," William C. Singleton III (*www.blackplanet.com*) wrote: "In another photo, a Confederate flag hangs behind a member in blackface and Afro wigs." This was not a new event in academia. In 1968, the *Temple University News* (March 27, 1968:3) reported that Tau Epsilon Phi brothers presented a blackface show at their group sing. And from *The Emory Wheel* (Emory University, April 14, 2000), Jada L. Barksdale responded to the use of blackface by Kappa Alpha:

> One issue that I think that the administration as well as the student body needs to recognize is that this incident is only one in a long list of insensitive, racist acts committed by members of the KA fraternity. I understand that they are acts of individuals, but since no effort has been made by the

fraternity to publicly punish or even restrict the behavior of these individuals, then I think that it is only fair that the entire fraternity be sanctioned.

Nor was the Auburn incident an isolated one in 2001. *Yahoo.com* (November 13, 2001) reported in a piece entitled "Miss. Students Expelled from Frat":

> Two University of Mississippi students have been expelled from their fraternity after an Internet photograph showed one dressed as a police officer holding a gun to the head of the second, who was in blackface. Similar steps were taken in Alabama by two Auburn University fraternities whose members also were photographed at parties in blackface—one with a noose around his neck, others wearing Ku Klux Klan robes.

Blackface is a symbolic cultural creation or artifact. It has a special meaning to a society that has used race and gender to construct a dominant understanding of white masculinity and manhood. Recent decades have seen an increased emphasis on the different meanings of masculinity and how these impact male identity and development (Kimmel and Messner 2001). A major aspect of scholarship on manhood and the "masculinity crisis" attending various social, political, and cultural changes has been the recognition that race and gender help to define what it traditionally means to be a dominant white male heterosexual (Bederman 1995; Horrocks 1994, 1995; Ipsaro 1997).

In "Media Blackface: 'Racial Profiling' in News Reporting" (September/October 1998, *www.fair.org/extra/9809/media-blackface.html*), Mikal Muharrar observed: "Examples of issues defined in blackface and subjected to a racial profile include the black drug abuser and drug dealer, the threatening and invasive black criminal, the black welfare cheat and queen, and the undeserving black affirmative action recipient." What is this resurgence of blackface all about? Is there any significance in the absence of discussion in these articles regarding the bunny-outfitted white females in several of the pictures? Why were they present? What did they symbolize? Why were their identities (their faces were blotted out) concealed? The white females in bunny costumes (theirs is a silent presence) seemingly do not need comment. Yet a comment is merited, especially since their faces were often concealed by the censors. But even if the absence of comment on white female resubjugation and complicity was not examined, the judiciary's role in this entire affair was noticed.

In what seemed like days, the judiciary rushed to defend the fraternity men. The judge insisted that they be reinstated because of a First Amendment right. This is uncannily reminiscent of the U.S. Supreme Court's snatching George W. Bush from the fire in 2000. Some saw the irony. Shawn Ryan of the *Birmingham Post-Herald* reported: "It happened with the frat boys at Auburn. It happened a couple of years ago when Atlanta Braves pitcher John Rocker shot off his mouth. People said Rocker was being denied his First Amendment rights when he basically denigrated every ethnic" (November 26, 2001).

There are many ways of understanding this situation. These rationales point to the "underside" of a white male identity crisis. The question of white identity in the current millennium is important here, as some scholars have appreciated. Joe L. Kincheloe went to the heart of the matter:

> The white identity crisis is real and cannot simply be dismissed as the angst of the privileged. While it is in part such an angst, it is also a manifestation of the complexity of identity as class and gender intersect with race/ethnicity, an expression of the emptiness of the postmodern condition, and an exhibition of the failure of modernist humanism to respond to the globalism engulfing it. . . .
>
> The pain of the perception of a new psychological disprivilege within an old privilege gnaws at contemporary white people. . . . The new disprivilege emerges from the increasingly valued concept of difference and Whites' lack of it. (1999: 11, 15)

This is a remarkably simple idea, but its simplicity partially conceals its significance not only for a pedagogy of whiteness but also for the basic business of "reaching" the humanity of the other. I turn to this theme again in the final chapter. Next I outline the subjective complexity of the "disprivilege" that Kincheloe described.

White Male Identity as Subjectivity and Stereotype

Wassup, Dr. Gresson—the maverick? Just seeing how things are going. This semester is pretty tough or maybe it's the professors. I was talking the other day about my field experience with my class and I used the word shit. . . . My professor told me to watch my language—can you believe that? Anyway, I don't think that my teachers enjoy my comic relief like you did last semester—do I stop being myself? Write me back if you get the chance.

I got this e-mail message a few months ago from one of my former students, Mark. I really like this young man, and I think he likes me as well. Actually, I find him remarkably similar to myself and many of the young African American males I have known over the years: bright, assertive, kindhearted, but sometimes vulgar and abrasive. But most of all, he wants to be "himself." What distinguishes this young man from me and these black youth is his racial-ethnic identity: lower-middle-class Irish Philadelphian. Because of his racial identity, Mark's question is a bit ironic: without changing himself, he may have to change his major from education, as indeed he later did. Yet as a white male with great potential, he will not have to make the major changes in self he feels pressured to do. This is because the main adjustment he is being asked to make is class oriented. That is, the academic environment he has chosen asks that he minimize or drastically curtail his free expression of behavior associated with being "white trash". But the inner tension he expresses is not unrelated to more powerful identity crises. Most notable of these, in my view, is the resurgence of blackface, which brings us to the matter of mourning. I call the process "dwelling in the surrender" and take it up more fully in chapter 4. What is the relevance of this mourning to white male identity?

At *crouch@patriot.net* is an article entitled "Why White Boys Sing the Blues: Lott Explores 'Racial Cross-Dressing.'" It is partly a review of an event:

> Eric Lott, Professor of English at U. Va., spoke to a packed hall at Swem last Thursday about "Racial Cross-Dressing and the Construction of American Whiteness." He treated antebellum minstrel shows, Elvis, Mick Jagger, Vanilla Ice and Lee Atwater as one continuous phenomenon, which is significant not as racism or exploitation, but rather for what it reveals about whites' notions of whiteness and blackness. To Lott, these "blackface" performances show a white male "fascination" with the color line, a self-conscious desire to assume a black identity temporarily. Lott described this sentiment as natural, not because white Americans somehow lack the earthy, casual virtues they attribute to blacks, but rather because they define certain painful and pleasurable experiences as black in order to maintain an artificially "respectable" white self-image. Lott pointed out that minstrel shows began in the 1840s, when women's Victorian standards of morality were becoming increasingly powerful in white society. White males reacted, like Huck Finn, by seeking opportunities "to be Negroes together."

I have described elsewhere (1995) how many white males have felt like the real victims of oppression and generally have appropriated some aspects of oppression discourse to publicize their pain. We might point to the "woman as nigger" and "white power" slogans of previous generations. Lott and others remind us as well of a longer history of white male identification with "the Negro" in a group setting. It is important to understand that in many life circumstances white males may participate in this form of group identification. Whether fraternity men or "boys on bikes" or "rednecks in the wood," a shared reading of "blackness" enables them to locate themselves as white. In the epilogue, I return to this topic as it pertains to the rise of so-called multiracial American society. Here my point is that blackface has resurfaced in twenty-first-century America and signals a crisis in white male identity. This crisis is both symbolic and substantive. It is symbolic because the cultural ideas of racial domination have been undermined by vast global changes. For instance, consider Asian Americans. In his essay "Up Identity Creek," Jeff Chang (see Joseph Harker *The Guardian*, *www.guardian.co.uk*, March 6, 2002) explained:

> If overeducated Asian American men—myself included—spent the eighties whining about being portrayed in the media as effeminate geeks, and bemoaning the loss of "our women" to white dudes, we are straight hoo-banging in the nineties. Now we can watch Jet Li kicking white ass on the big screen. We win all the DJ contests. We roll in the flyest Acuras and we run Silicon Valley. Cellular phone companies want our money because we've come a long way, baby.

The substantive dimension of the crisis is political and economic and based in the immorality characteristic of capitalism. This system simultaneously exploits racial difference and rejects it for profit. Capitalism loves no one. The fusion of the two dimensions of white identity crisis is illustrated in the Enron scandal: privileged white males sacrificed thousands of, notably if not solely, middle-class white Americans for their own gain. The erosion of confidence in white economic institutions exposes millions of whites to a fate shared with minorities and other underprivileged people. It is in such a context that people traditionally become vulnerable to various forms of fascist backlash behavior. The earlier-discussed resurgence of blackface is a case in point. But there is something powerful that has been, and still is, taking place among millions of white males: a realignment that has aggressive features but is ultimately aimed at establishing a *terra firma*.

Conclusion: "The Gaze" and White Pain

Growing up a working-class black man in the Old South, I have always understood the tensions attending eyeballing whites, especially white males. I knew that that to look a white male in the eye said something to him about him that he didn't want to see, hear, or own. Just yesterday, I was reading a new book on women's dress in nineteenth-century America as a radical, rhetorical statement. It made a parallel observation about women who entered the public domain, who became public speakers, who left the parlor and

> chose the platform, a location no longer passive and controlled for private scopic pleasure . . . In order to understand the fear associated with this active look of women speakers, it is helpful to examine the depth of convention that forbade women to return men's look directly. . . . Assuming the privilege of looking directly at another undermined the power structure that helped to keep gendered and class hierarchies in place. The lower classes, especially slaves and free blacks, and women were expected to make eye contact only with others of their station, not with their superiors. (Carol Mattingly 2002: 137–38)

To make eye contact with a superior is to explode a collusive bond, to renounce the ground beneath the other that holds him or her aloof. To make eye contact amounts to refusing to mirror to the other a desired, acceptable self. Throughout this book, we will return to the fact that white pain ultimately pertains to a subjective experience of loss symbolized by the loss of priority with respect to "the gaze." Master may look upon slave still; but now the slave may also look upon the master. But it not just looking that causes a crisis.

The "look" implies a pre-determined knowledge of the other; the white person (especially the white man) thus becomes a stereotype. The bitterness generated by this new status, this dislocation from the position traditionally labeled "the Man," has many familiar expressions: "go ahead, blame the white man/race for everything," "yes, I'm a white man and I oppress everybody."

To challenge this unwanted trivializing of all whites as the same, various alternative strategies have been employed. Finding others to reassume the central role of gazed upon negative object is chief among these strategies. For instance, since 1970 white women have been disproportionally represented as the "bad gender" in movies (Hedley 1994). The dominant negative racial image has already been described by the "angry white woman" cited earlier in this chapter: the black male.

The power of the media to chain this image of "minority evil" to "white innocence and civilization" was depicted in a recent documentary featuring Bishop Desmond Tutu and the African American historian John Hope Franklin. In this video, young people from Africa, Europe, and the United States met in Senegal for a week of racial discussions and healing. One observation made in the documentary was that all the youth from Africa and Europe—both white and black—shared one dominant image of racial evil: the *young* black male.

America's Atonement is ultimately the renewal of the vision of and belief in an *innocent whiteness*. From this perspective, beyond all the reasons proffered for the recent war against Iraq, America's recovery of "something" lost on 9/11 is the enduring reason we have resisted all criticism and pleas for alternatives to war. The billions and billions of dollars President George W. Bush is asking for the war, tax cuts, and the rebuilding of Iraq are aspects of this atonement. Atonement is felt to be critical to regeneration, recovery of a cherished view of self. The attainment of this renewal and regeneration is a massive and complex one. In the next chapter, I focus on its operation in schools and universities—the academy.

·2·

WHITE STUDIES AND RACIAL
PAIN IN THE ACADEMY

Do not plague me with this "whiteness" business, you Hegelian robber.
AUTHOR'S FRIEND, 1994

Prologue: The Problem of "Whiteness"

Early during the preparation of this book, I received the preceding comment in an e-mail from my closest friend and adopted brother, Robert, in response to an article I had written on the racial themes in the movie *Forrest Gump* (1994). The allusion to Hegel comes from a passage I first shared with him twenty years earlier when we both were doctoral students at Penn State University. I had found this remark in the preface to *The Concept of Irony* by Søren Kierkegaard. Kierkegaard, the father of existentialism, supposedly uttered it to the members of his master's thesis committee in nineteenth-century Denmark.

Rob and I both felt the sentiment deeply because of our constant battles with "the establishment." Over the years, we have often repeated these words to each other about members of the establishment whom we felt were harassing us about some academic or public matter. We had never before said this to each other, though; this was a first. I did not feel overly bothered by the comment because we regularly chided each other about something. Our friendship, moreover, was far too strong to be undermined by such an incident. I mention it here only because I think it illustrates the complexity of contemporary discourses on whiteness.

By associating me with the Kierkegaard incident, I believe Rob was expressing his concern with the discourse of whiteness. In addition, he was alerting me personally to the painful aspects of whiteness talk. Rob's response to my talking about *Forrest Gump* as "the call back to whiteness" leads me to the question, Why does the notion of "whiteness" infuriate so many and lead otherwise progressive, fair, white scholars to identify it as yet another instance of "political correctness"? I believe one under-examined answer to this question is the relation of "whiteness" as a concept to *white pain*. It is this relationship that I examine in this chapter.

The Nature of "Whiteness" and Its Tensions

"Whiteness" is a fairly new concept or idea in certain circles, namely, parts of academia that deal with analyzing power in America. Since most economic, military, communicational, political, and cultural power is dominated by persons and groups identified as "white," it now is common to speak of "whiteness." Of course, the control of most public or collective power (versus personal or individual power) has always rested with white Americans. What makes the concept so special in 2003 is that various social and political actors in the United States and elsewhere have realized the importance of *naming* this power. Most people do not regularly come into contact with either the word *whiteness* or the people who care to use it in their presence. The word per se is important only to a very small collection of scholars and political activists. My friend Rob belongs to this group. But this man differs from most other white academics I have personally known with respect to matters racial. For one thing, he has included personal reflections on racial matters in some of his scholarly writings. A brief examination of his thoughts, many contained in his quasi-autobiography, *Adult-Child Research and Experience*, is helpful to us in gaining a partial understanding of the whiteness issue and the matter of racial pain.

"Whiteness": A Personal and Professional Legacy Examined

When I asked Rob about his e-mail message to me, he expressed a number of concerns regarding the notion of "whiteness." For him, the notion

- Seems to identify white men as evil incarnate;
- Suggests whiteness is essential to white men;
- Ignores power as the real focus of liberation and oppression discourse;
- Ignores the interchangeability of race and gender when describing the destructiveness of power;

- Fails to be clearly identified as a "metaphor" rather than "something real";
- Promotes the continuance and intensification of racist conflict in the United States and elsewhere.

Rob is a sensitive, decent, courageous humanitarian. We have been friends and colleagues for more than thirty years. We have lived and traveled together, both in the United States and Europe. He has seen me in good and bad moments, as I have him. Furthermore, he has given much thought to being "white" and expressed some of his reflections in an important book on the professional and personal significance of alcoholism. In one place, for instance, he notes:

> Neither was I socialized into *identifying* with a heritage; I could not therefore understand people who identified with their social origins. When I went in the Army, I heard people talk and joke about various ethnic minorities. This, too, I thought made no sense. Were they not people just like me? What does where your grandparents were born have to do with the person standing before me?
>
> While working on my masters degree, I was required to take a course on race relations. The seminar was composed of about 15 students. Some were "Mexican," some were "Jews," some were "Italian," some were Black, and some were "American Indian." They all discussed their ethnic heritage and said how proud they were to be what they thought they were. I boldly told them that they made no sense. It was clear that I had insulted them. I did not mean to; I was just trying to figure it out. When asked what ethnic group I belonged to, I told them I did not belong to any group. They then asked what national origin I was. I said I was born in Portland, Maine. Okay, then, they said, so you do identify with being an American. I said "no" I did not. They asked if I considered myself a Mainer. I said I could somewhat identify with that.
>
> I knew what they wanted to hear. I told them my grandmother had once mentioned that I was Irish, English, and a "wee bit" of Scotch. They asked if I was proud of it. I responded by saying they might as well ask me if was proud of being a human from the planet called Earth. I completed the seminar without emotionally understanding what it was all about. (Haskell 1993: 105–6)

Rob attributes his lack of "emotional understanding" to his personal biography rather than his racial privilege. Hence, the subtitle of his book is *Personal and Professional Legacies of a Dysfunctional Co-dependent Family*. In this way Haskell explains his refusal to acknowledge difference as a personal matter of identity. But I see his capacity to insist—without major consequence—that race and ethnicity did not matter as racial power. Indeed, Haskell partially reveals the deep psychological character of whiteness when he describes his own growth beyond the provincialism inherent in much racial liberalism:

> Years later while teaching in Harrisburg, Pennsylvania, I interviewed Aaron, a candidate for a position on the faculty. He had black skin (actually it was brown). There was considerable prejudice, as well as "liberal" acceptance of Aaron. He was a brilliant fellow. I thought of Aaron as simply a man who, by virtue of accident of birth, happened to have black skin, so that if he would wash it off, he and I would be the same. It was only years later that I realized that my "color blindness" was a kind of prejudice, too: People are different because of their experience of growing up in a different culture. For some 18 years now, Aaron and I have been brothers. Aaron is also an ACOA. Many of my feelings, thoughts, values, beliefs, and behaviors have been marginal to the society in which I live just as it would be if I now went to live with Eskimos. When a person lives psychologically outside of his culture to a considerable degree for a sufficient period of time, and being told that he should be like everyone else, he begins to question his own sanity; he must be crazy. I had these feelings as a child. I made a vow I would not go crazy. There were times when I thought I was going crazy. During those times, I would beat my fist against the wall, breathe deeply, sing to myself, rock furiously in a rocking chair radio up loud and concentrate on each word. I was, in fact, having what is called a panic attack. ACOAs may have more than their share of these. (1993: 103–4)

Haskell understands the privilege aspect of his position. He introduces both a personal and a racial confession: his disassociation from the group-constructed and group-enforced mandates of racial identification. Because of this refusal to buy into whiteness, Rob experienced periods of panic; however, unlike most persons so stricken, his anxiety was caused by never being told that standing alone was OK. This emotional isolation reveals the irony in his behavior: making a choice that could be made effectively only if he remained invested in "whiteness" as a positive identity.

In the earlier passage, Haskell revealed his limited appreciation of the racial dimension of an otherwise nonracial identity. Perhaps a bit of this attitude persists in his outrage at my *Forrest Gump*. If he had no investment in whiteness, perhaps he would not have felt as much of the sting. I don't identify this quality as racist per se; it is an orientation that can appear even if one rejects the brutality of racism. Rob, for example, showed this while we were graduate students at Penn State University in the mid-1970s. The occasion was the day after a young (white) male had opened fire on an unsuspecting public on the campus of the University of Texas. We were walking past the graduate library (Pattee) and talking about some shared racist experience (over twenty years Rob and I had shared more than a few such incidents) when he said, "Aaron, if I were a black man, I would get on top of Pattee with a rifle and open fire on the public too." I replied, "You sound just like a white man."

For years, Rob did not understand my meaning; perhaps even now he only partially appreciates my meaning despite his knowledge that events similar to those he was describing are almost always committed by white males. Beyond the statistical story, I was trying to share with Rob a fact—true for the time—about *racial position:* role-identified, random destructiveness due to personal pain is something one largely learns. It is often facilitated by a sense of *entitlement.* Not everyone who feels entitled or otherwise stigmatized commits the act, but rarely does someone outside the entitled group commit certain kinds of destructiveness. This is why until recently women rarely killed men, or blacks killed whites just because they were angry at the world.

In addition, and this is a source of black male pain, whatever their circumstances and fantasies, most minorities have understood in the very marrow of their bones the folly of expressing their racial pain by means of random retaliation. During the height of the black power movement in the 1960s, historians Rudwick and Meier wrote the following:

> It would appear that both in the World War I period, and today—and indeed during the ante-bellum era and at other times when manifestations of violence came to the fore—there has been a strong element of fantasy in Negro discussion and efforts concerning violent retaliation. The Black Muslims talk of violence, but the talk seems to function as a psychological safety valve; by preaching separation, they in effect accommodate to the American social order and place racial warfare off in the future when Allah in his time will destroy whites and usher in an era of black domination. . . . Du Bois and others who have spoken of the inevitability of racial warfare and Negro victory in such a struggle were engaging in wishful prophesies. And Negroes have been nothing if not realistic. The patterns of Negro behavior in riots demonstrate this. In earlier times, as already indicated, those who brought guns in anticipation of the day when self-defense would be necessary usually did not retaliate. And Negro attacks on whites occurred mainly in the early stages of the riots before the full extent of anger and power and sadism of the white mobs became evident. (1969: 412, 417)

Elliott Rudwick and August Meier are discussing here the rhetorical aspect of racial rhetoric, notably black threats toward whites. In this passage, they also identify a major component of the enduring racial shame and pain that blacks, particularly black men, feel: the fear of physical, social, and economic retaliation by white men. This racial pain and knowledge partly underlay my inability to do anything more than fantasize about hurting masses of whites, even though, in theory, I am certainly as capable as Rob is to imagine the wholesale slaughter of others in retaliation for my perceived racial pain.

This is an important point. Whites seem to believe that minorities want to retaliate against them with catastrophic consequences. For instance, an entry in my diary from September 3, 1990, reads as follows:

> Today I asked the students their response to the *Time* article, "Beyond the Melting Pot" [April 9, 1990: 28–30]. I was struck by the strong "fear" this essay caused for a few of the students: the observation that America is increasingly a multiracial and multicultural society; and that white Americans are becoming a demographic minority, seems to elicit fears of retaliation. One young woman said: "I didn't like the article because it seems to say that we are going to get paid back for what we did to blacks, Indians, and other minorities in the past. I don't think that I should be penalized for what happened in the past." I tried to reassure her and the others who might share her feelings. I said the black psychiatrist, Frantz Fanon, found [1968] that the dreams of mentally fatigued French soldiers in Algiers [Africa] often reflected a parallel concern: they often dreamed that they were being overwhelmed by hordes of blacks and destroyed in the manner western movies portrayed Native American massacres of white settlers. But these were just fantasies and fears: formerly oppressed people of color have rarely retaliated with kind toward their oppressors. Some students seemed consoled by my words. However, I could tell that most of the class did not understand the reason for fear a few had shown—not because minorities were as benign as I inferred, but because they can't even conceive of a society in which whites are not everywhere and in charge of everything.

Despite the historical insistence that "the other" is less than fully human, whites conceal a belief that the very humanness of "the other" must be defended against. Although various animalistic images—monkey, baboon, gorilla—have been conjured up to define "the other," what is feared is the expression of the full humanity of "the other." The duplicity implicit in white racial history strangles whites when matters racial surface, and the inability to confront this duplicity leads to the contradictory visions that permit some to claim the superiority of "whiteness" (Bork 1996; Kirk 1993) and others to insist that equality and justice permeate the land (D'Souza 1995).

The irony is the peculiar conversation, or emotional logic, that under-pins this duplicitous discourse. On the one hand, it is characterized by de-nial, but on the other, by despair. The denial is that racism and oppression are alive, and so whites are *innocent*. When incontrovertible evidence is shown, denial gives way to despair, a fear that these tendencies can never be overcome. But there are times and ways for rehearsing this racial inher-itance, as Rob indicated in his autobiography. Sometimes when talking with Rob, I would push his button by seemingly essentializing white evil and destructiveness. This was not my intention; words sometimes are "bad" vehicles because they say both what we mean and more. Over time, I came to see that many whites—and perhaps Rob—can tolerate the par-ticular, situational, historical destructiveness that whites have perpetrated as a part of whiteness only if it is clear that (1) they personally have disen-gaged from such "white evil" and (2) that "white evil" itself is a variant of human evil, no worse than that in Asian or African history.

Personally, I have been able to grant the first part of the "demand": in-dividual whites are no worse than individual blacks, yellows, greens, or whatever. The second part is more difficult—historical circumstances being different—and requires a more qualified response. I have often used the example of male/female battering to explain my reservation or qualifi-cation. While it may be true that women hit men as much as men hit women, as some argue, it is not true that the physical and societal conse-quences for female batterers are, *collectively*, the same as those for male batterers. Likewise, human destructiveness and oppression in bygone times may have been as vicious, systematic, and unrelenting as that asso-ciated with recent Western civilization. Still, it cannot match the destruc-tive power unleashed on the world in the twentieth century alone. The ideology identifying white European culture as the world's best and God's chosen (Bork 1996; Kirk 1993; Slotkin 1973) argues that it has contrib-uted unique gifts to the world. There is much truth in this belief, but there is much nontruth as well. In particular, this ideology has often debunked alternative realities. It is chauvinistic; it is arrogant; and it is defined in op-position to "the other": homosexuals, women, and nonwhites.

As one consequence, millions of white youth committed to a demo-cratic ideal are compromised when introduced to a multicultural dis-course. This is seen by the relative elision of "white ethnicity" through the creation of whiteness as a racial identity. In a class assignment, a young white male of Irish, German, French, and Spanish background wrote, "I feel somewhat cheated from not being able to learn anything about my mother's side of the family and their cultural heritage. A large part of this

may be that their family has been in this country since before the revolution so they feel completely American." This young man continued his
autobiographical reflection:

> One experience that I do not enjoy is that it seems like when I look into my
> heritage over the last couple of hundred years I feel a sense of shame. I feel
> this because unfortunately the Europeans feel superior to all other races and
> have done many awful things to a lot of different ethnic groups. This has
> caused me much grief because I enjoy history and different cultures and do
> not understand how we could feel this way and do the things that we did.
> This leads to one of the values that I hold that I do not want to but feel has
> been ingrained into me through out the years of my life and the generations
> before. This value is the value of supremacy, or thinking that I am better
> than every one else. I do not like having this but can see it at different points
> in my life. This value is key to understanding a lot of what the people with
> my ethnicity do.

Understanding the inability and undesirability of "erasing" everything
white, some scholars sensitive to the dilemma of a new generation of
white youth call for clarifying the "good and bad of whiteness" (Giroux
1998; Kincheloe et al. 1998; Nelson and Villaverde 2000). These scholars
differ from those who believe whiteness to be so perverse that it must be
scrapped. But what is it precisely that these "recovery school of whiteness"
scholars want to salvage? What can be identified that is good, admirable,
and prideful?

I have come to see that these questions are especially important in
classrooms trying to transform the limiting, undemocratic, and inhumane
aspects of whiteness. In the multiculturalism teacher education classroom,
for example, I have tried to help my students access this transformative
agenda through the use of autobiographical exercises. The following ex-
cerpt is from the essay of a bright, self-assured young woman. Pay particular attention to her effort to balance the things she is proud of—the
things that she has identified with and internalized as parts of her own
identity—with her ever changing awareness of social oppression:

> I was raised under the principle that hard work will ultimately lead to suc-
> cess. My Irish-American paternal grandfather grew up in the coal regions
> of Pennsylvania during the worst of the Great depression and my Dutch-
> English maternal grandfather lived on a farm in Indiana. Both came from
> humble beginnings and worked hard for every penny that they made. My
> father was raised by his school teacher parents in a modest home in

Pennsylvania, working both after school and on the weekends. He graduated from Villanova and began working at an entry level job at du Pont. His good work ethic and sharp people skills allowed him to advance on the corporate ladder. . . .

Success is not solely measured by accumulation of wealth, but rather by happiness. I can see now why my parents are both very successful. They have not only achieved economic security, but have enjoyed raising three terrific children over the past 25 years. Instilled in my brothers and myself are the family values of hard work and ambition. For example, in the first grade, I was labeled and stigmatized with dyslexia. Rather than let my learning disability get the best of me, I worked extra hard to catch up to my peers. By the third grade, I was on reading level and by the 6th grade I was above reading level.

I understand that by being "white" my family has always had social privilege. After serving in World War II, it was a lot easier for my grandfathers to get jobs than their "colored" counterparts. In addition, it was a lot easier for my father to get into college and then land a job in corporate America than it was for minorities at the time. To reframe this, in times of adversity, one could always count on their "whiteness" to help them out. That still holds true.

My ethnicity could be characterized as "white" upper middle class. Since almost everyone in this country considers themselves to be middle class, then that might not narrow that down too much! Furthermore, I use the term "white" for lack of any better [word] to use. I do not regard my race in everyday life and understand that there is no absolute American "whiteness." . . . I have financial stability, a good education, and a traditional white nuclear family. I am empowered in all areas but one—I am still only a woman.

Being aware of my ethnicity has allowed me to be conscious of racial and ethnic prejudices in our society. For example, I went to racially and ethnically diverse public schools growing up. I saw that the "white" students had better teachers and more money was spent on them. I am not ignorant to the social injustices in our school systems. I noticed that "black" students were always expected to be very athletic and not very academically oriented. White students were expected to perform better academically.

This young woman helps put flesh on the essential meaning of whiteness in its distinctiveness. At base, whiteness pertains to privilege codified in terms of a color code and working to increase and retain power as symbol and substance. From this view, much of white existence is no better or worse than any other. Moreover, while it may not be "Christian," "Democratic," or "just," the use of whatever means necessary to attain and retain power does not differentiate whites from others. Thus the transformation of American society does not solely pertain to changing or modifying whiteness. Still, it does require some changes among whites concurrent with other social changes (Butin 2001, 2002).

What I am suggesting is that the fusion of white identity with power over several centuries and the continual renewing of this fusion through racism are the conditions that must be changed. It is the resistance to these twin tensions that causes white pain. I felt this tension in the preceding passage, and I have sometimes felt it in my relations with my friend Robert. In one sense, this pain is due to an inability to believe that whites can be loved by nonwhites for their positive "white" qualities. But whites are loved and they do have many wonderful, inspiring, awesome qualities, just as all other humans do that have grouped and named themselves "the best."

It is important to understand that others, including minorities, share this chauvinistic proclivity. It is inevitable, I suspect, that racial and ethnic identities convey a commingling of positive and negative elements. For instance, a young Jewish student completing the same exercise and clearly alert to the complex historical representation of Jews in "the Gentile world," accessed his ethnicity in the following manner:

> Judaism has also taught me the value of continuing the Jewish tradition. Judaism is a minority religion and as the rate of inter-marriages increases, the Jewish population is decreasing. Being Jewish is an important aspect of my life, and I want to share this with my children. For me, spreading the wisdom of Judaism, its teachings and its traditions with future generations, is something I feel very strongly about. In hundreds of years, I want Judaism to be alive and growing. . . . I have accepted many other values from Judaism . . . the importance of all humankind, the equality of all people, the capacity of all people to improve themselves, the importance of sharing and giving to the less fortunate, and the freedom of choice and responsibility for one's actions. I use these teachings and ideals of Judaism in my everyday decisions and actions.

These reflections are complex, as they imply and conceal broad historical and political strokes and invite a diversity of perspectives and passions. For that reason, many see the academy as the wrong site for stimulating diversity discourses. Using the rubrics of "academic integrity" and "scientific neutrality," the depth of the white pain propelling much of "human science" remains understated and underexamined. The complexity here may be seen in the response to whiteness studies.

The Paradox of Whiteness Studies: The Teaching of Alienation

One of the unavoidable consequences of social change activism is the possibility that those seeking social justice for the oppressed may participate in oppression. This is an ancient idea, certainly traceable to biblical passages such as "Let he who is without sin cast the first stone" and classical references such as "Physician, heal thyself." The topic of whiteness studies illustrates this very well. One Internet site declared, "White Is a Color Too" and contained the following:

> A front-page article in the *Wall Street Journal* last month certified that "whiteness studies" has arrived. The burgeoning academic field—informed by both thoughtful race theory and liberal Caucasian guilt—has already spawned hundreds of acolytes; more than 70 books (according to the Center for the Study of White American Culture Inc.'s Web site; sub-specialties such as white trash, suburban resentment, and male ethnography; and a national conference held at the University of California this April 9, 1997). Among the field's primary objectives is exposing the privileges that come with being white in order to make them go away. The *minnesota review's* [*sic*] current issue is titled "White Issue." This fall, *Transition*, a Harvard-based journal of global culture, will publish its own white issue, in which nonwhite scholars will weigh in on whiteness.

This is an exciting extract; it also is a powerful indictment of whiteness studies. First, it reports a negative article from the *Wall Street Journal*, and second, it rehearses and expands that negativity. The forcefulness of the negativity is achieved by putting down the Ivory Tower. By emphasizing the academy's cultural climate—as reflected in the ideas of subspecialties, elite institutions, academic journals, and so forth—it succeeds in reaffirming the Us/Them difference. This approach trivializes the field, whose goal is to expose "the privileges that come with being white in order to make them go away." How ironic, the passage seems to laugh, that whites who are presumably privileged academics dare undertake the task of exposing themselves as whites as a means of de-privileging themselves. Yes, it is a laugh—and so Harvard gets over on Minnesota by permitting nonwhite scholars to get in on the white bashing.

This depiction of so-called whiteness studies has been presented to the public in a way that fuels an already deep-seated sense of racial victimization. Consider the following letter to the editor of *The Chronicle of Higher Education*. Entitled "Taking Pride in Being White," it states:

Seldom have I read such bias and distortion in a respectable publication as that reported in the article "Lifting the Veil from Whiteness: Growing Body of Scholarship Challenges a Racial Norm" (September 8). I do research on prejudice and know it when I see it. I favor fair treatment for all races, ethnic groups, etc. This fairness has to include whites as well as others. If *The Chronicle* article correctly reports their views, the scholars all seem hostile to whites and white identity. The only one who is clearly out front in his prejudice is Noel Ignatiev, the Harvard University lecturer who edits a journal called *Race Traitor*, with the motto of "Treason to whiteness is loyalty to humanity." The other scholars seem to be serving the same purpose, but with a false facade of objectivity. It is bad enough that whites are the victims of a quota system called affirmative action, which causes them (especially white males) to be discriminated against, to work (as I have in the past) for an incompetent supervisor, etc. Now you have academics putting them down. And there is an irony to all this.

The irony is that of all the races and ethnic groups, whites have a record that is extremely good. The intellectual contributions of whites throughout history are impressive, and they have a low crime rate as well. The crime rate among blacks is very high, as is the amount of illegitimate births, which is now reported as 68 per cent of all black births. H.I.V. and AIDS are growing among blacks and Hispanics, while they are leveling off or declining among whites.

We should want to keep the positive aspects of white culture, while of course getting rid of the negative aspects. More people should be proud of being white, given the great achievements of whites. Yet due to change in the immigration laws, it is quite possible that early in the 21st century, whites will become a minority in the U.S. This can be changed if the immigration laws are changed, but it will not be changed if we have more and more propaganda against whites.

A few years ago I would not have imagined writing a letter such as this one. I felt the main problems were discrimination against blacks, Hispanics, women, etc. But it is clear that it has become all right to discriminate against whites, and people have to start speaking up and taking a stand. Most whites have little racial identity as whites. It is time that changed. As the article makes clear, whites are under attack for being white, despite their valuable contributions to civilization. (October 20, 1995: B3)

For me, the power of this passage is the pain it gives off. This man, a professor of psychology at a state university in the South, believes himself to be a fair, decent, and racially knowledgeable professional. Furthermore, he clearly has had personal experiences with unfairness based on "preferential privileges." Most of us can identify with him in this regard. We have known unfairness and we know ourselves to be largely fair, decent human beings. It is precisely this narrative power that makes this passage so much more powerful than the whiteness studies scholarship it critiques. As I showed in the previous section, whiteness studies fail to satisfactorily convince most people, especially those who are unsympathetic, that they have something meaningful to share. On the contrary, whiteness studies increasingly serve the interests of racists, widening the racial division so deeply embedded in American culture. They do so because despite their goodwill and sound scholarship, whiteness studies are characterized by *duplicity*. What do I mean by this statement? Certainly, whiteness scholars are largely sensitive, decent, and courageous. I mean that, contrary to their intention, whiteness studies enable whites to disavow racial privilege even as they assert, as whites did nearly two decades ago, the need for white power. Hence, this writer can say: "The irony is that of all the races and ethnic groups, white have a record that is extremely good." This seemingly necessary position thus converges with more racially chauvinistic positions such as that of Russell Kirk (1993) who stated unabashedly in *Anglo-American Culture* that whites are the superior race and ought to be on the top. Such positions also show convergence with more widely publicized commentaries such as Murray and Hernnstein's *The Bell Curve* (1994). Because of the efforts of recovery scholarship like this, contemporary whites are able to claim a racist ancestry without being characterized as racist; hence the preceding passage tells us that nonwhites are the really bad characters. Whites do not have to face their unique history of racist savagery and its unprecedented qualities, and so lynching and other forms of human destructiveness have been kept away from the image of white = civilized (Bederman 1995).

Racial misery and decay are deep inside white culture, but control of the public representations of pain and pathos fools even whites. Yesterday, a white neighbor and I were talking about black self-hate. He indicated that he had read about this phenomenon years earlier but had never really encountered the phenomenon in his all-white world. I noted that whites had their own self-hate dynamics, pointing out that the neighbors living down the hill from us in the trailer camp are called "white trash" and "trailer trash" by other whites, both working-class and middle-class whites. He was momentarily dazed and gradually smiled and softly admitted, "Yeah, I guess you're right. . . . I never saw it like that before."

What collective unconscious tendencies account for this blindness or myopia? How does it play itself out in teacher education and the challenges facing white teachers in diverse settings? I believe an important and useful clue is given in this brief autobiographical reflection:

I've been fortunate to have lived a fairly diverse life up this point. I was born in Washington, D.C., while my father was attending Howard Medical School. He once told me that at the time (the early 60s), students who weren't either Black or Jewish were the minorities on campus. . . . My family moved around a lot until I was almost six years old. We went from Washington to an area of San Diego known as Spanish Harlem to the Bronx in New York. In all of these neighborhoods, we were the only White family. Even when we lived outside of Philadelphia, we were the only non-Italian family. Until we moved to Aspen Hill (a community slightly north of Rockville, MD), I'd never seen people with blonde hair or light skin other than my sister, my mother and myself. When a Black family moved into our neighborhood, my parents had to explain why my sister's best friend never came out if we were playing with Desmond. I was nine years old, and this was the first time I'd ever experienced prejudice. Elementary school was filled with kids who looked just like me and I had now become aware of that fact. I started to understand the derogatory comments that relatives on my mom's side of the family (from "down South" in Virginia) sometimes made. My father's family, predominately Baltimore Jews, was even worst [*sic*] because they denied what they were doing.

One theme in this passage is the collusive nature of racial identity construction: one has to grow into one's identity through specific experiences. And in a world with contradictory messages about racial equality and the like, we see repeated instances of this problem even in the most liberal, decent families. To more fully appreciate the character of white pain in the academy, I now share a particularly though not singularly painful experience in my own academic life.

A Failed Multicultural Education Textbook: Whiteness, Gatekeepers, and the Academy

In 1993, I was asked to write a multicultural education textbook. The idea was to produce a volume that would be both marketable and groundbreaking. To be marketable, the book would address the traditional topics in foundations of education in a manner currently absent from most introductory textbooks. On March 2, 1993, I wrote to my publisher: "By helping students to contextualize their own experiences as citizens in terms of the evolving Teacher Reform crisis we can enhance both their learning and their future teaching. It is precisely this contribution to their education that Foundations has been struggling with for the past two decades."

The publisher was pleased that I had chosen a narrative format emphasizing the interplay of autobiographical voice among diverse speakers. In his return letter, I sensed both excitement and expectation: "My cursory examination of an hour or so makes me very hopeful about the prospects for what you are attempting; you certainly argue convincingly for a book of this kind, at this time" (March 10, 1993). I was feeling fairly proud of myself at this point; I was particularly excited that my publisher felt positive about my narrative style. My elation was short-lived, however. His letter of July 23, 1993, began thus:

> I am generally pleased by the response of our reviewers. It seems to me that the story-telling aspect of the manuscript is going well, many of the pedagogical learning aids are useful and attractive, reviewers generally think you write well, and they applaud the book's multi-cultural emphasis. There are, however, one or two things we need to work out before I think I can offer you a contract. These issues are related, and they touch on the strong presence in this book of the author's own voice and own experiences, particularly touching on race issues. Although multi-culturalism is one of the book's main virtues, three or four reviewers indicate that you have dealt with race too much, too strongly, or too polemically for the book to find a wide national readership. Because what you have written is clearly in places very personal, it is hard for me to tell you exactly how to cut back the discussions that most worry reviewers. I would say the discussion of the circumstances surrounding your birth is the sort of thing that reviewers found too personal, perhaps too loosely connected to a discussion of education in general, and too "hot" to suit a text with broad commercial aspirations.

The "groundbreaking" aspect of the textbook was to be achieved by having a working-class, minority author, and I had hoped to establish my "pedigree" by "writing myself into the text." Accordingly, I had tried to illustrate the power of narrative by telling the story of my birth: I was the first African American baby born in Norfolk (Virginia) General Hospital in 1947. My mother had gone into labor and was rushed to this white hospital by the paramedics who feared for her—and my—life. The hospital staff first rushed to admit her, then stopped—they had never delivered a black baby at this hospital. So my mother remained in the hallway until her physician, a Jewish refugee from Hungary, came and threatened to bring murder charges against the hospital staff if my mother or I died.

I had told this story partly to indicate why I felt a strong identification with Jews and how heroic some whites were even during pre-1960s America. I had also told the story as a way of clarifying the importance of "indigenous" storytellers. I had not counted on the strong antipathy that the story stimulated in my white reviewers. My publisher was correct; even reviewers favorable to the book complained:

> I think that the author initially raises several thoughtful points regarding minorities, especially Blacks, in our society. He must be careful, not to allow this to degrade into defensiveness. We cannot continue to blame the White race for past travesties. It is time to move forward with such thinking and to speak from equality, not to simply continue to blame the White race for all shortcomings of our society. I have no problem with the author's writing style. I do have a problem [with his] attempting to use this book as a platform for White race bashing. Clothing that purpose in a foundations text is wrong. It surfaces in both chapters and is inappropriate.

For me, this reviewer's words were especially painful because he liked my work. Clearly, I had failed to say what I wanted to say in a nonproblematic way. But I did not immediately see what I had done wrong. Perhaps because so much had changed since the pre–civil rights era, I no longer had a sixth sense about these matters. In fact, it took some time for me to understand how telling the story of my birth, *sui generis*, constituted blame of the white race for all human shortcomings. True, I did contextualize my birth in the racial relations dominant in 1940s Virginia. What this reviewer's comments told me was that any attempt to speak outside the designated discourse caused white pain. Hence I am now expected to "speak from equality" and avoid putting whites on the "defensive."

Another reviewer, from the University of Wyoming, labeled me a "social reconstructionist" and declared:

> The bitterness in the author's autobiography is understandable but his admittance that his life as a teacher is inextricably tied to his unhappy past would make it almost impossible for him to be objective as an author and a teacher. . . . Resistance as a result of guilt feelings on the part of White students is counter-productive to the creation of empathy. A genuine feeling of care for *all* children is a necessity for the teacher of today and tomorrow. . . . Students are not to be blamed for wrongs they have not committed.

Equating good or effective teaching with the absence of painful remembrances or present oppressiveness is very telling in this passage. Presumably, my "bitterness" places me outside of the mainstream realities from which "healthy" and "effective" teachers are chosen. It is a well-established principle of power relations (Wilden 1988) that the more powerful persons often are better able than the less powerful persons to use language to support their claim to the "moral high ground" precisely because power remains at their disposal. In this case, this reviewer had power over me because ultimately most reviewers, authors, publishers, and education consumers share more features with him than with me. Thus, even as he "laments" the conditions that may have contributed to my "bitterness," he is able to label me "tainted" and "flawed" and hence unsuitable for teaching. For him, my experiences, passion, commitment, and, yes, cognitive competence are liabilities rather than assets. He—and this remains a dominant feature of contemporary whiteness/Americanist apologetics—actually believes that he and other members of the dominant social order are "non-tainted" and "objective." In addition, it seems to me that implicit in my reviewer's comments is a belief that somehow I can or should become so "value neutral" that I do my students a service by not placing before them competing realities and inviting them to choose, thereby "making it ideological" rather than "academic." This "request" or "logic of dominance" means leaving aside my own reality. Accordingly, my own knowledge and experience—the presumed basis for an alternative professional voice—is transformed into merely a difference of skin color.

From a critical perspective, however, by separating students (and others) from the social world they inhabit and help construct, this reviewer continues in that tradition of teacher education that treats evil, destructiveness, and the like as reifications, that is, as independent entities constructed outside reality and more powerful than the people giving them reality. Still, a critical view can often fail to console someone marginalized even as he seeks to "do the right thing." I was devastated by these critiques.

But what had I expected? I had expected criticism of specific weaknesses in my writing style, mastery of the literature, and even my reasoning. I had not, interestingly, expected a personal assault. This is because, I must confess, I had been prepared to soften my views and knowledge in order to enter the big time. I had even been shrewd enough to ask the publisher to confer with me before sending the material out to reviewers in order to gain a better feel for them as my audience. He had written in response, "I will honor your request and I will look through it myself and chat with you about it before sending it to reviewers" (March 10, 1993).

But he didn't—and the gatekeepers of official knowledge were not fooled. They saw that I wanted to reach the young, white leaders of tomorrow, to challenge them to not merely assume equality reigns but to accept the contemporary consequences of past acts of wrongdoing and to see how such a past persists even into the present. The gatekeepers said no!

It may be interesting to note that the loss of agency I reported experiencing in the preface began during this period of preliminary work on the textbook. Only later did my book on recovery fall on hard times. Indeed, as I write this, I am forced to wonder whether the removal of *The Recovery of Race in America* from the publisher's list didn't merely finish a process begun much earlier. Whatever the source of my sense of loss, the various reviewers' comments served to confuse, disorient, and ultimately anger me. Anger could come only later because so much of the destructiveness came through the partial praise for my effort. For instance, one reviewer praised the work as a novel:

> If I were using this textbook, I would add my own personal experiences as well as those in my class. I would also enjoy spending some time in class to discuss "narrative power." Nevertheless, I do believe that some students would not have the level of maturity required to get beyond the fact that there may be an attempt to indoctrinate them in what they may perceive as fostering "political correctness." Furthermore, when compared to traditional textbooks in foundations, it is extremely rare to find an author who writes from a personal perspective with the same degree of passion, if any passion at all. I must admit, however, that I read Chapter 1 as I would read a novel. My interest level was extremely high.

The ambivalence of this reviewer is perhaps more accurately read as ambiguity: he was less torn between two attitudes or emotions than alert to the presence of a strong tradition disdaining—even denouncing—passion in scholarly work. Nor is this a racial matter in the most simplistic understanding of "racial." I recall vividly that decades earlier, my department head at Brandeis University, asked me, in exasperation, why I closed my first book, *The Dialectics of Betrayal* (1982), with a plea for—and admission of participation in—scholarship wedded to passionate commitment. This man was a black African, albeit one most vulnerable to the influence of colonialist values and standards.

Still, while committed to passionate scholarship, I was true to the assimilation's impulse in many American minorities, trying to shift my cultural lens or perspectives to be accepted, to be mainstreamed. Hence, when the next publisher—who had already given me a contract and cash advance—asked me to prepare new chapters for another review, I shamelessly and thoroughly erased all traces of "blackness" from the manuscript. I was so effective that one reviewer even identified me as "an experienced White male academic with a vast knowledge of minorities." He went on to ask, "Is that important for me as a reader to know?"

I later shared with my white female editor—again to my shame—my observation regarding this shift in perceptible voice in the text. In response, she wrote, "I agree with your sense of the reviews regarding the

African-American issue that arose in the proposal stage. My sense is that it is no longer an issue. As long as you are not perceived as a 'dead, White male' (!) we're probably somewhere in the ballpark on this" (April 10, 1995).

I understand that she was trying to be cute or humorous. But she failed, and so did the partnership. I had gone far in trying to enter the mainstream, to win acceptance to the club. To do so, however, I would have to change, negate, and suppress my real story, my real self. I somewhat redeemed myself intellectually and morally, if not financially, through the publication of *The Recovery of Race in America* in 1995, when much of this textbook discussion was occurring, and later through my withdrawal from this particular textbook project. Still, for several years after this experience, I occasionally looked through the reviewers' comments and lamented my ability to "deliver the goods" that might have catapulted me into national prominence and won me other lucrative writing contracts. But my greater lament is that my white colleagues all too often have little or no faith in young white youth and their capacity to grow beyond the duplicity, deceit, and dishonesty of their forebears. To wit, I recall that one reviewer wrote cynically:

> While encouraging moral reflection about, for example, societal injustice authors need, it seems to me, to take special care their own judgments and values are subjected to critical review. I do not think this is the case in these two chapters either by the choices of content or by the writing itself. . . . The student essays do not show the quality of thought for inclusion in a text. . . . I immediately thought here's a case of the student giving the instructor what he wants to hear.

I am certainly aware that people may say what they think a more powerful person wants to hear. Indeed, this has been an essential part of my racial inheritance: saying what "The Man" wants to hear regarding himself and his goodness in a world suffused with pain generated by his nongoodness. But I believe that very few white students are so frightened by the few minorities in power positions that they systematically succumb to brown nosing. Still, this critique raised for me some questions regarding the role of the minority multicultural educator, especially in a predominately white classroom.

Over the years when I have reflected on these comments, I am repeatedly struck by a dual irony: (1) a black man might be so positioned in the academy as to merit a serious response from the gatekeepers and (2) much pain and fear underlay their comments. The latter fact was especially powerful, since neither my writing ability nor my reasoning powers—traditional points of attack against minorities in academia—were cited as problematic. Beyond this, I was struck by a common clue to the crisis produced by a radical educator like myself for these and presumably other educators and majority-group students. Any critique of contemporary racial practices feels like a personal attack on the very character of the white individual and an attempt to dismantle everything known as self and valued as important to the collectivity.

Two things stood out for me especially in the preceding comments. First was the idea that white students "turn off" and refuse to receive communications that fail to represent "positive racial relations." Second was the intimation that racial passion born of racial oppression, such as my autobiography conveyed, precludes one from being an effective teacher of majority-group students. Having taught for more than thirty years at several predominately white institutions and practiced psychotherapy for nearly as many years with majority-group members, I reject both these suggestions. White students do not necessarily turn off when exposed to less than positive stories about racial relations. Nor do one's racial wounds necessarily disqualify one as an effective educator. Still, both suggestions do contain elements of fact and wisdom. And it is within the painful experiences of minority students in academia that we can often see the limits and possibilities of blaming the victims of oppression for both their victimization and their resistance to it.

Wide Wounds: Terrorism and Critical Thought

If suffering is the lived experience that corresponds to the concept of alienation, a psychology of suffering would have to understand guilt, anxiety, depression, or hysteria as suppressed social relations. (Lyman 1981: 58)

The refusal to talk about Vietnam and to deal with its excesses, like the refusal to consider what precedes terrorism, invites mythology—an "axis of evil"—and so the opportunity for critique is thus killed, silenced. In chapter 3, I take up an observation made by Kincheloe and Staley in 1983 on the rise of anticritical thought in schools on the Vietnam era. Here I anticipate that discussion with a further reflection on the matter of a democratic, anti-oppressive pedagogy.

One critical flaw in the insistence that the democratic teacher cannot act against oppressive attitudes and actions in the classroom—if they are presented as subjective understandings and individual opinions—is that it

results too often in precisely the kinds of judicial decisions now being presented as First Amendment rights, even though they are blatant acts of racism. Consider the case of the Auburn University students who not only
were reinstated after their expulsion by university officials but who also
now have a multimillion-dollar lawsuit against the university for interfer-
ing with their right to carry out racist actions at the university and have
them placed on the Internet.

This attitude, interestingly, relieves resistant students from having even
to entertain the alternative voices and curricula of nonoppression. For instance, today I received two interesting e-mails. One was from the dean of
the Commonwealth College thanking my campus executive officer and
everyone for successfully hosting President George W. Bush's visit to our
campus to speak on urban education. The other e-mail came later, from a
former student. For me, the two e-mails suggest two separate cultures and
worlds that seemingly never meet or mesh yet remain linked in a dance of
agency. But to understand what I am trying to say, it is perhaps helpful to
know that I might have met President Bush had I not been in New Or-
leans at a conference on education. To have met a living president, whatever my politics, would have been something indeed. But this is precisely
the problem. I have great problems with the structure and operation of
many institutions and actors in our society, including presidents. So to
surrender my strong political concerns in a display of starry-eyed loyalty
and hero worship would indeed have been difficult for me. But I know I
would have been like putty in front of President Bush. So I was not disap-
pointed in not meeting him despite my institutional pride that he chose to
speak at Penn State.

To appreciate more fully the irony and profundity of my ambivalence,
you might benefit from reading the other e-mail I received that day (it was
sent to me two days after Bush's visit). I include it here in full:

> This is Ninat and Daisy [pseudonyms for these African American females]
> and we just wanted to tell you about what happened in our Children's Liter-
> ature class, get that!!! Greta [a young, white female transfer student from
> the main campus] decides to tell our teacher that this program [Urban Edu-
> cation] is ineffective and our Fall semester with you was a waste of time.
> Ninat and I could have killed her and we let the whole class know that it was
> on them if they got nothing out of that education. I let them know that just
> as they had more expectations of you, you had many more expectations of
> them and that they missed the ball for the most part. Ninat came to your de-
> fense immediately, stating that she learned a lot and this is the best way for
> her to learn. Liz [a middle-aged white mother and wife] was pissed, quiet in
> her seat. She did blurt out by asking if Greta had read any of the books that

you assigned. Of course she said yes, but she doesn't even come to class this semester. Ninat and I really just want to let you know that we "got it" and that you had a great impact on our intentions as teachers. We could afford to learn much more! from you and hoped that you would teach a class that is unassigned in the upcoming Fall. I now understand that this may not be a good idea. I am up to my neck in anger with them and I just plan to ride the next semester out. We would be sitting here for days writing if we told you about everything that has been going on. Some of our classmates hate you and that is painful to accept. Now they hate us too, so we stand together and that's cool. I would give nothing to be amongst those idiots!!!!!!!!! I just feel sorry for the children that they may one day teach. Your teaching was reflective of the power that our children need; sublime and understanding. Thanks again and we'll talk to you soon. We want to find some time for us to meet, maybe this summer in Philly or up here, whatever. Let Ninat know by e-mailing her back. I can't seem to get mine to work.

What is so ironic and significant to me—receiving this e-mail from these two beautiful, brilliant, and committed young sisters—is that their angry e-mail arrived just days after Bush's historic visit to our campus. The two black women feel racial pain. The two white women also feel racial pain. What are the odds that Bush addressed this pain or the relation of teacher education to the educational changes he hopes to inspire and introduce? I am certain that the conversations with Bush were sanitized and thereby promoted a vision of nonresponsibility for the urban educational plight that he came to address. In short, innocence is the dominant understanding of why so much despair and destructive energy surround the urban educational context.

I admit that my teaching is politicized. Roland Barthes (1973) calls "mythology" a kind of "depoliticized speech" because it fragments meanings by distorting and manipulating language so that everybody wins, and nothing really challenging occurs because the emotionally charged material is neutralized. Although one senses that something important may be happening, one detects a subtext beneath the words. Although I resist it, I regard such teaching and scholarship as relevant to the new resistance to the "posts" perspective on anti-oppression.

It is not surprising, however, that even before the academy adopted an official, scholarly position on this perspective, society struggled with ways of silencing the new voice of the voiceless (Gresson 1995). A remarkably telling illustration of the structure—Molefi Asante and Deborah Atwater (1986) termed this the "rhetorical condition"—of minority-led discussions about anti-oppressive education and cohabitation was presented by Derrick Alridge. Alridge studied with me at Penn State

University in the mid-1990s. Vigorously courted by several major institutions, he returned to his home in the South where he joined the University of Georgia. Often during his first years of teaching, he would share stories with me and compare notes on our respective teaching experiences. Like me, he began collecting student responses to his pedagogy because of their unique historical and instructive multicultural insights. Recently he published a chapter in which he recounts his early years of teaching:

> Teaching is another area of scholarship and knowledge dissemination where black scholars face the issue of the silencing of black voice. I recall a few incidents dealing with my "black" perspective and voice while teaching my first social foundations of education course at a predominately white institution. The class was about 99 percent white. In teaching the course, I relied heavily on my own worldview as a black man growing up in the American south. I also used my black voice in discussions related to our topics of educational history and policy. While I received good evaluations from the class in terms of my knowledge of the subject matter and organization of the class, I was somewhat surprised at the students' response to my being "too black" or black-focused in the dissemination of the information. I later realized that no matter how objective I thought I was, many of the students still received my lectures as too black and felt that I was blaming them as individuals for the educational inequities of blacks in the United States. (Alridge 2001: 197)

It has been said that in many ways reality mimics fiction; it also may be said that the same applies to the academy and the "real world." Alridge's experience is reminiscent of my own as a black man whose entrance into the later half of the twentieth century found me no longer blatantly subordinate to whites but nonetheless subjected daily to blatant racist assaults and perennial paranoia with respect to white intentions toward me. Hence the peculiar double bind that Alridge and I share as black male academics is the call to teach as black men with the simultaneous insistence that we be "raceless."

The point is bigger than academia: what does Condoleezza Rice or Colin Powell, as blacks, bring to the Bush administration that is informed by a racist heritage? If nothing is gained racially by their presence other than their presence, then it is truly as my former student and close friend Susan Mason declared in 2000: "Multiculturalism is Dead! Now everyone gets to sing . . . it's just that everyone will have to sing the same song."

Conclusion: A Voice from the Past

I have not resolved a good part of the paradox of the minority educator. I revisit it each semester when I struggle with what is implicit in so thoroughly de-racing myself that I am perceived as "an experienced White male academic with a good knowledge of minorities." What does it take to be an effective minority teacher educator in the multicultural classroom? Too little attention has been given to this question, and I return to it in chapter 4. There I take up the recent focus on the oppressive potential of anti-oppressive education. Here I would like to anticipate that discussion with an affirmation: the democratic educator must indeed bite the bullet, so to speak; this includes, at times, pursuing truth with a long view—saying things to students, even things that they find challenging, that one understands to be "true." In this one makes, or rather, accepts the risk that one may violate the democratic ideal.

Such an attitude means, at times, that one must go for years without validation. One may also, in a hostile academy, find oneself marginalized and subject to criticism from those protected by and supportive of that oppression interstitial to the academy. Still, I do find occasional validation, such as this e-mail from a former student that I received just a few weeks ago:

> My name is Dave and I graduated from Brandeis in 1983. If you remember me then you are even brighter than I thought you were. I just wanted to let you know that I often think of you as the events of this world compel me to remember you and your teachings. I often joke with my brother, who also had you as a professor, that you missed your calling to make "big bucks" with the "Dialectics of Betrayal Part II—the Anita Hill and Clarence Thomas Story" or "Dialectics of Betrayal Part III—the Johnny Cochrane and Christopher Dardon Story." You "coulda" been some big shot on Geraldo. But I guess you'll just have to remain an outstanding professor. You were a real maverick at Brandeis; I liked your style. Lastly, *Dialectics of Betrayal* was a real "pain in the ass read" driving me to the dictionary every other sentence to look up all these fifty dollar words that you told us you were compelled to use in order to be accepted by the academic elites. It took me a couple of years thereafter to fully understand your thesis and as a result I have a better depth of understanding of many racial issues in this country. I hope you enjoyed my thoughts—you're great at what you do. Goodbye and God Bless, Dave

This young man—he must be nearly forty! Gad, that makes me an ancient—was apparently one of the students I taught at Brandeis University in the early 1980s. It is truly awesome that he should reconnect with me in

2002. I only vaguely recall him or his brother. And it seems that he has not kept up with my career since 1983 or the books that I have written since then. Of course, that doesn't really matter to him or me. I can only presume that he was reaching out for his own fading youth and trying to connect to the past and gain some control over the chaotic times we now endure in America: attacks by enemies on our homeland, a war on terrorism and Iraq, military tribunals, the "American Taliban," escalated conflict in the Middle East, and a volatile economy.

I, too, am searching for control, however short-lived or illusionary. What this young man's words and the other commentaries I receive from time to time offer is a soothing validation of a life lived at the margins. Ironically, the book that Dave spoke of, *The Dialectics of Betrayal*, is very instructive in a certain, bizarre way. Although it never won any awards or sold anything like the numbers that *The Recovery of Race in America* did, it remained in print for eighteen years! Why? Perhaps because it dealt solely with minority pain, it was an OK book. White pain was not emphasized. Yet both pains are real and in need of soothing.

If we understand that the racial critique of whiteness promotes white pain as well as racial understanding, then perhaps we can begin to see that the mediation of white pain is a major initiative of the recent cultural wars that academics so often write about. In the next chapter, I turn to the question of mediation as a way of getting closer to an understanding of contemporary shifts in the multiculturalism discourse. Specifically, I illustrate one way in which women in general and society in particular seem to have promoted such an agenda as part of a culture-building project that I have called "the relearning of patriotism."

I use the so-called yellow ribbon movement and the Tom Hanks hit *Forrest Gump* (1994) to illustrate the main arguments of this chapter. I indicate how the yellow ribbon movement associated with the 1991 Gulf War was co-opted to help revisualize the soldier as a positive white male icon. In this pursuit, I argue that the social radicalism of the 1960s converged around a common notion of "the enemy," white male power; that the white male soldier came to symbolize this power; and that the recovery of popular warmth for the white male soldier became an essential symbolic dimension of the recovery of a more or less unified country, one such as we have now in the aftermath of September 11, 2001. The argument I make is that both women in general and white women in particular have been used repeatedly since the 1970s to depict a certain set of preferred gender relations. Moreover, symbolically—and presumably substantively—these representations promote pain reduction and a kind of recovered "normalcy" in the realm of social relations and social justice.

· 3 ·

MEDIATING WHITE PAIN

Ritual Recovery, Yellow Ribbons, and Patriotic Wars

The war in Vietnam threatened to tear our society apart. And the political and philosophical disagreements that animated each side continue to some extent. It has been said that these memorials reflect a hunger for healing. Well, I don't know if perfect healing ever occurs, but I know that sometimes when a bone is broken, if it knits together well, it will in the end be stronger than if it had not been broken. I believe that in the decade since Vietnam the healing has begun. And I hope that before my days as Commander in Chief are over the process will be complete.
RONALD REAGAN (1984: 1825–26)

The final lesson of Vietnam is that no great nation can long afford to be sundered by a memory.
GEORGE H. W. BUSH (1989 INAUGURAL ADDRESS)

Introduction: Self-Examination versus Group Healing?

The various equality movements of the 1960s and 1970s were a partial reason for the rise of multiculturalism and diversity initiatives in the United States. Vietnam symbolized the nation's struggle with its own creed and promise of democratic inclusion and godliness. Multiculturalism and diversity demands were the forbidden fruits of this struggle. And as we have seen in the previous chapters, these initiatives brought with them considerable pain for many whites, even as other whites provided both leadership and other forms of support for these initiatives. In the 1980s, healing the wounds of this struggle—Vietnam, black power, the antiwar movement, the feminist movement—was critical.

In 1983, Joe Kincheloe and George Staley wrote in a special to *USA Today*, "Only a decade after the Vietnam debacle, public schools are once again equating critical inquiry into the formulation of American foreign policy with anti-Americanism" (1983:30). The refusal to look too deeply beneath the surface is a common human trait, and despite its greatness, American democracy does not necessarily challenge this human propensity. For this reason, the "critical inquiry" that Kincheloe and Staley correctly encouraged actually flew in the face of the national objective described by Ronald Reagan and George Bush: healing the cultural, social, and political split associated with Vietnam and the social activism of the 1960s.

President Ronald Reagan understood this very well, and on November 11, 1984, when Frederick Hart's bronze statue of the three infantrymen was unveiled and dedicated, he spoke the words opening this chapter. This memorial was a mediating force. *Mediation* is defined as standing in between, acting as a connection between two otherwise separate, conflicting entities, ideas, or circumstances. Hart's memorial was offered as a compromise to those who felt that Maya Lin's memorial, *The Wall*, failed to promote healing for many Americans, especially those who felt we had failed to win the war because of weak leadership and the subversion of the antiwar movement.

Kincheloe, Staley, Reagan, and Bush bring us face to face with a complex matter: how do we balance our ideals and the pragmatics of social life? This is a perennial issue for a democratic society. Indeed, at the same time this chapter focuses on the Vietnam–Gulf War period, 1972 to 1992, we are currently waging a "war on terrorism" that revisits the dynamic tensions of these earlier times. I will return to this connection later in the chapter. First, however, I offer one perspective on the manner in which white pain has been mediated in our society. In particular, I try to answer the question, How does the white male, separated from the community through his hegemonic or collusive elevation to dominance, find his way back to at-oneness with the group? This question is critical to understanding how power dynamics interface the diversity discourse reopened during the so-called radical 1960s, the period lamented by Max Rafferty and others like him.

One way of beginning this discussion is to return to the white male voice. To a considerable degree, white males are correct when they take a stand against the white male bashing that portrays them as the initiators and sole perpetuators of white male dominance in society. This observation both highlights the subjective reality of individual white males and exposes the collusion of others in constructing society. Anthony Ipsaro noted that white males become powerful because of society's collusion:

But let me tell you a secret: Most men in most cultures have no sense of their power! They have remarkable power. Since that power is inherited through cultural gender expectations rather than earned, it is an invisible mantle. Although each male has his own brand of masculinity, all men share a relationship that fosters an alliance of domination and subordination. This is achieved through practices that exclude and include, exploit and reward, intimidate and reaffirm. The entire cultural system supports, reaffirms, and colludes with white males to keep them in power. Yet, most white males do not think of themselves as belonging to a powerful, elite group until others label them that way. (1997: 14)

The weak and strong together construct power. Others have said much the same thing: Dorothy Dinnerstein in the *Mermaid and the Minotaur* (1976) and Franz Fanon in *Black Skin, White Mask* (1967) described how women, Jews, and blacks colluded with Euro-American racialism to perpetuate white male domination. Mary Daly also brilliantly described the hegemonic drama with respect to gender:

The Myth Masters are able to penetrate their victims' minds/imaginations only by seeing to it that their deceptive myths are acted out over and over again in performances that draw the participants into emotional complicity. Such re-enactment trains both victims and victimizers to perform uncritically their preordained roles. Thus the psyches of the performers are conditioned so that they become carriers and perpetrators of patriarchal myths. In giving the myth reality by acting it out, the participants become reproducers and "living proof" of the deceptive myths. (1978: 102)

In the epigraph opening chapter 4, a graduate student describes the white females in her women's studies class as afraid to challenge the white males. Perhaps this was the case, but female collusion in such incidents is an alternative reading of the situation. This perspective was developed by Kathleen M. Blee in *Women of the Klan* (1991), on racism and gender in the 1920s, and by Ruth Frankenberg in *The Social Construction of Whiteness* (1993), on white women's role in the construction of white identity. Together, these works recognize and record specific ways in which white women can contribute to the continuation of white male power even as they resist it. This process was evident in the rise and ritualization of the so-called yellow ribbon movement to mediate white male pain.

The Yellow Ribbon Movement and the Mediation of White Pain

Yellow ribbons were used widely during the Iranian hostage crisis, but the practice was first adopted to welcome the returning prisoners from Vietnam, inspired by the 1973 love song by Tony Orlando and Dawn, "Tie a Yellow Ribbon round the Ole Oak Tree," about a returning convict.

GERALD PARSONS (1991: 11)

In November 1979, Muslim revolutionaries seized the U.S. embassy in Tehran, Iran, and took fifty-two Americans hostage to symbolize the initiation of political and religious war on the "imperialist infidel" America. The president, Jimmy Carter, a Democrat from the South, was perceived as too weak and accommodating to tackle this aggression in the same way as would, say, Theodore Roosevelt, hero of American imperialism in the 1890s. When he was elected in 1976, Carter symbolized the redemption of the South, its recovery from the economic exile imposed as a result of losing the Civil War. But by 1979, Carter's failure to obtain the hostages' release symbolized America's failure in Vietnam: the failure of God's chosen country to vanquish a weaker, "evil" enemy (DeSousa 1984; Hill 1984). It was this Iranian crisis that led to the first national ritualization of the yellow ribbon Movement. Penne Laingen, wife of one of the American diplomat hostages, made a huge bow from several feet of yellow vinyl upholstery material and tied it around an oak tree in the front yard of her home in Bethesda, Maryland. In a seminal essay on the evolution of the yellow ribbon as an American folk icon, Gerald Parsons, of the Library of Congress's American Folklife Center, recalled:

> On the CBS broadcast of January 28, [1979] Penelope Laingen . . . was shown outside of her home. . . . "It just came to me," she said, "to give people something to do, rather than throw dog food at Iranians." I said, "Why don't they tie a yellow ribbon around an old oak tree? That's how it started." (1981: 9)

Over the next decade the yellow ribbon periodically appeared at sites of American shame and defeat, notably when American military men were killed. Various authors have emphasized the heterogeneous motives of Americans with respect to the yellow ribbon symbol and the tension and conflicting meanings it encoded. Still, beneath this disruptiveness lurked the common recognition that the yellow ribbon emotionalism was emanating from precise sources and directed toward a precise mission. Penne Laingen fused a personal pain and need with a collective pain and myth. To say that the movement began with her gesture is inaccurate, but her gesture did become a collective motive and mission.

Like many women, Penne Laingen enacted the ritual encoded in the song. In so doing, she gave life to a myth, a desire. For many, perhaps most, Americans, her gesture, like that of the unnamed woman in the song, was cathartic and touched something deep within them. Although we did not know the history of the song's beginning, we probably associated it with Vietnam veterans. Some women made the connection right away. In March 1992, the American Folklife Center received a handwritten letter which reads as follows:

> The July 15, 1991 issue of the *Library of Congress Bulletin* contained an article which implied that the Folklife [Center] believes that yellow ribbons were first used to welcome home prisoners during the Iran hostage crisis. However, I recall hearing on "Casey Kasem's American Top Forty," a nationally syndicated radio program, that yellow ribbons were used to welcome home some Vietnam POWs. According to Mr. Kasem, several people who had done this told the singing group Tony Orlando and Dawn about it during a concert of the group's.

The yellow ribbon song was published in 1972, and Tony Orlando and Dawn's recording of it was released in 1973. Thus began the public oration of the plea from Vietnam and shortly thereafter began the public ritual of yellow ribboning. But to present this chronology of events as a natural unfolding begs the issue: how did such actions become the basis for the recovery of the American soldier as sacred icon? To answer this question we must consider the place of guilt and shame in the lives of Americans generally, and men and women specifically, since the start of the Vietnam War in 1965.

Vietnam was not only America's greatest military failure but also America's most unpopular war. Furthermore, the traditional ambivalence of women, particularly mothers, about their sons going off to war surfaced as a gender problem. Although a smaller part of the larger antiwar sentiment, the gender resistance to America's military presence in Vietnam was the most painful part of the domestic crisis of that time. Perhaps this was because so many subissues were linked to the gender crisis, all of which found resonance in the word *rape*. This word struck at the heart of the American male/soldier's self-concept. Indeed, one of the recurring themes of Vietnam era literature and film was the rape scene. We see the important connection of rape to women's role as antiwar demonstrators in Larry Heinemann's Vietnam-focused novel *Paco's Story*. The following quotation depicts a veteran's fantasy revenge on a college female, a symbol of feminism and the suffragist yellow ribbon tradition:

Been waiting for one of those mouthy, snappy-looking little girlies from some rinky-dink college to waltz up and say . . . "You one of them *vet'rans*, ain'cha? Killed all them mothers and babies. Raped all them women, di'n'cha". . . "I ain't putting out for you, *buster*. . . ." Okay by me, girlie. . . . 'cause I got seventeen different kinds of social diseases. . . . And when this happens—this conversation with this here girlie—I'm gonna grab her up by the collar of her sailor suit . . . , slap her around a couple times, flip her a goddamned dime . . . and say, "Here, Sweet Chips, give me a ring in a couple of years when you grow up." (Heineman 1986: 156)

A number of works, largely fictional, addressed the role of women during the Vietnam War (Jeffords 1989: 199). A recurring theme in much of this literature has been the failure of women to provide support in the form of an unconditional acceptance of war and male behavior in war. From the perspective argued by feminists like Mary Daly, on the one hand, unconditional acceptance of male aggression such as displayed in war is an act of female complicity. On the other hand, the refusal to accept war as necessary and inevitable might well represent the kind of nonsupport displayed by antiwar demonstrators. If such apparent nonsupport is allegorized in the female and if it truly generates the kind of fictional and actual misogyny depicted earlier, might women not share a parallel negative self-regard? Indeed, evidence from both World Wars I and II suggests women often accept responsibility for the entire society for failing to show support and remain faithful to military men. According to some scholars, women have been made to feel responsible for both the start and loss of war (Gilbert 1989). Female guilt and traditional atonement rituals— grieving and mourning—converged in the yellow ribbon movements of 1979 and 1991 to become a male recovery ritual. Many women felt guilt for the antiwar movement. Some of the women who became Vietnam nurses entered the war because of such guilt feelings. Similar sentiments, in part, stimulated the yellow ribbon movement of 1991.

The Gulf War of 1991

In August 1990, Iraq invaded Kuwait. America quickly responded, identifying the invasion as an act of aggression against both a peaceful country and the world. America then guided the United Nations in establishing an international war offensive, with President George H. Bush's administration orchestrating the nation's and Congress's compliance with the UN mandate. The United States declared war on Saddam Hussein, and by May 1991 Iraq had been bombed into submission.

People's Magazine began its commemorative issue on the victory in Iraq with the following reflection:

> When it started last August, Iraq had the fourth largest army in the world, and the United States was said to have little stomach for war. When it was over, seven months later, Saddam Hussein's military machine was no longer an international threat, and the United States had purged itself of the ghost of Vietnam. . . . Wrapped in a yellow ribbon, this package [special issue] contains the unforgettable stories of the heroes (and, yes, a few of the villains) of the short, sharp war that helped a country feel good about itself again. (1992: 44)

To "feel good about itself again," America went to war. This idea was not the common rationale for the war in the days and months before victory had been achieved. Many people believed that the war was truly about Iraqi aggression and its threat to the world's economic and military stability. Some felt that the United States' need for oil underlay the decision to declare war on Iraq. But by the war's end many understood the redemptive motive, whatever its economic and political underpinnings: the nation's need to feel good about itself again. From this view, the Gulf War helped complete the meaning of the Vietnam War, particularly the reunion of the Vietnam veterans with other Americans. (The "war on terrorism" and current occupation of Iraq by American forces has again raised the specter of doubt regarding motive and method.)

This convergence of past and present—failure in Vietnam and apparent victory in the Persian Gulf—was an orchestrated redemptive drama. It did not just happen; it evolved over a decade or more. The war in the Gulf was itself a fulfillment of the psychological needs of the American people as much as it was a political need of the government. The yellow ribbon was a vehicle, albeit a source of ambivalence, for this healing to be acted out. The ribbon was everywhere, on trees, fences, car antennas, light poles, and doors of houses, barns, and churches. Although these rituals signaled that the yellow ribbon pertained to more than tradition building, even in 1992 the redemptive significance of the yellow ribbon ritual was underexpressed. War, the traditional American ritual of regeneration, was not yet acknowledged as a recovery activity, nor was the ribbon identified as a redemptive icon:

> The war with Iraq was a specific social context that raised deeply disturbing questions that were addressed through this folk art. The assemblages also dealt with other cultural and social contradictions: opposition to war versus support of the troops; loyalty to country versus abhorrence of war. The flags

and yellow ribbons addressed these issues, allowing for some personal expression through the manipulation of the symbols. The ratio of yellow ribbons to flag-related icons, the placement of the symbols, and the use of the
printed signs all helped to specify one's position on these issues. (Santino
1992: 31)

In this passage, Santino raises several important points. First, for most
Americans, support of the troops was not equal to support of war; it
couldn't be otherwise for a country that had failed to heal the deep
wounds associated with Vietnam. (Before the Gulf War, the nation had
been characterized as having no stomach for fighting because of the memory of Vietnam.) Second, the ambiguity of the yellow ribbon allowed for
the personalized narratives that Santino mentions. Third, the personaliz-
ing of narratives regarding war in visual form not only represented a potential repeat of Vietnam—sending multiple messages to the enemy—but
also heralded the replacement of a single metanarrative of war (traditionally symbolized by the American flag) with many competing and sometimes conflicting personal narratives of commitment and discontent.

The underexamined aspect of the war at home was the effort to shape
public understanding and values regarding the war. Even as I write this, in
2003, the country, having found its way back to Iraq, is trying to weave a
believable narrative of redemption through the discourse of an "axis of
evil." Of course, the drama in the Middle East, including Israel's refusal to
submit to a visit by the United Nations to areas in which it has perhaps
committed atrocities, mutes the American rationale for invading Iraq.
What is important here is not who is wrong or right. My concern is to
show the persistence of domestic-international issues that find the notion
of American interests intermeshed with racial and national identity-based
struggles around the world.

The complex issues embedded in this seemingly policy matter pertain to
the ways in which "American (white) identity" is both constructed and positioned vis-à-vis others at home and around the world. Although I will not
develop the discussion here, it is worth noting that returning Vietnam veterans connected much of their self-soldier identity to images of John Wayne
and the range of racial and national values with which he was associated. For
instance, Mark Gerzon (1982: 109) observed, "The Reagan administration
represented an energetic attempt to return to the 'John Wayne thing.' It
hoped that young men would once again idolize the Soldier."

But if one part of the white male's identity pain as a soldier and a man
derives from a militaristic or aggressive sublayer, another part derives
from a romantic sublayer. In fact, it is here as well that we must examine

why both aggression toward blacks and the embrace of the white bunny female occurred in the Web-site representations of the Auburn University frat men. Gail Bederman (1995) argued, in Chapter 2, that sexism and racism are intermeshed; similarly, Lois Weis (1995) found working class male identity development relies heavily on depicting the black male as the dangerous sexual aggressor of white females as part of his own wooing of white females. The Auburn frat men's fusing of blackface and playboy bunny seems to fulfill both Bederman and Weis's arguments. This fusion also points to the paradoxical nature of romance as ideology and narrative, and its relation to the lessening of white male pain. This fusion as well reveals the inevitable fusing of white identity with American identity. (As I note in the postscript, this linking of American identity with whiteness in a proprietary manner partly explains the repeated observation of a racial divide between white and black on various issues such as the recent declaration of war against Iraq.) Like blackface, romancing yellow is a racial ritual that supports the lessening of white pain.

Romancing Yellow and Lessening White Pain

Romance is a complicated matter in our society because romance is about idealism, hope, and "good feelings." We usually imagine a boy and a girl in love when we think of romance, as this image of a couple speaks to the ways that our society privileges or holds as natural, correct, and inevitable the coming together of male and female to create a family, clan, tribe, community, and even a nation. There is another side to the idea of romance, which is that it often conjures up images of betrayal, with somebody getting hurt by loving the wrong person or loving too deeply, that is, by being too romantic.

Who is romantic and who gets hurt can vary, as we know from books, movies, and personal experience, although the female is typically chosen as the one hurt by romance (Radaway 1987). According to the romance as a story form or genre, boy meets girl, they fall in love, boy hurts girl, girl loses boy, boy is enlightened, and boy returns to girl who finds love and marriage. Whatever the different attitudes toward this particular scenario, it is familiar and part of the way we separate male and female and understand the differences between the genders. To be sure, we humans create the meanings of these differences—as well as the differences themselves in many situations. Still, we largely accept, celebrate, and recreate these differences.

Because women are called on to render this service, it is probably why we do not want women in combat. Even though they may die in combat arenas, they do so while supporting the fighting men. This is an aspect of romance, present in much military art, announcing, "We support our troops!" Patriotism and gender are romantically linked to military action in this manner. Gaye Jacobson, credited with beginning the yellow ribbon movement of 1991, explained it this way:

> Patriotism had been missing from our lives ever since Vietnam. And, by God, we thought if we could anything to do about it, we would. The yellow ribbon signifies waiting for someone you love to come home. I saw it as the one symbol people would look at and understand. (cited in Santino 1992: 44)

Jacobson's movement repeated the one began in 1979 by Camilla LaSpada, founder of "No Greater Love." Writing in the 1970s, LaSpada revisited the site of both Gail McGruder and Penne Laingen when she drew the clear romantic underpinnings of the military scene:

> Historically, the use of ribbons or "colors" appears in many contexts. Medieval knights wore their ladies' colors as a sign of remembrance. American Civil War women were the first to tie ribbons (often yellow) to trees to signify their hopeful wait for the return of their men. Later, cavalry units adopted a yellow stripe down the sides of their trousers, to set them apart from other services. (personal communication, 1992)

The white female leadership in this ritualization of patriotism has been underexamined, but is pervasive in media about the yellow ribbon. There is evidence that independent individuals and groups began carrying out the ritual shortly after the song became prominent. I view this as the localization of the ritual. By "nationalization," I mean the adoption or appropriation of the ritual by the mass media and a network of myth producers. For example, Camilla LaSpada raised funds from various businesses in order to produce a massive number of yellow ribbon buttons that were then distributed nationwide. Both LaSpada and Jacobson felt that the yellow ribbon solved a crisis of identity. Other women also attempted to mediate the fusion of patriotism and soldier with American foreign policy and aggression.

> During the Second War, we always had a flag in the window or on the door. Then during this conflict war and all, they were putting up the yellow ones. I got tired of seeing yellow ribbons on the trees and posts. . . . I used the red, white and blue. I went to the florist and told her that I wanted a large red, white and blue bow and then I hung it with this wreath that was already done in yellow.

I interviewed this speaker in 1991. At that time, she was a seventy-year-old widow who lived alone with her dog in a small rural region of Pennsylvania. She supplemented a small fixed income with part-time work at a neighborhood food co-op. For her, the yellow ribbon movement was reminiscent of World War II: she had a brother who served in that war and she recalls that gold stars were placed in the windows of homes where a son or daughter had been killed in combat. For her, too, the Vietnam era was one of conflict, conflict left unresolved by the presence of so much yellow.

The failure of the media interpreters went far beyond oversimplifying the meaning of the yellow ribbons in actively constructing the preferred meanings. The war in the Gulf was not the only war waged during the winter of 1991. A "civil war" was also being waged on the home front:

> Sybil Roberts, whose nephew is in the Persian Gulf, was so angered by anti-war protesters at her door carrying petitions that she wrapped the columns on the porch of her Houston row-house with yellow satin, buried the facade under 14 giant yellow bows, and planted a sign in her lawn that read, "We support our troops" on [one] side and "Down with protesting" on the other. (*New York Times*, February 4, 1991, A16)

Few seemed to want to see the yellow ribbon as the redemptive ritual—an act of purgation and cleansing—it was, yet the redemptive theme found its way into the war rhetoric: a *New York Times* editorial described tying the ribbon around trees as "no frivolity, but pleas, prayers, and hopes made visible" (*New York Times*, February 4, 1991, A16). For example, the article about Sybil Roberts went on to observe that antiwar supporters also claim the yellow ribbon, that the cueing or compelling image is that of Sybil and her sign declaring protest as unpatriotic. For instance, the passage begins "whose nephew is in the Persian Gulf," a clause that serves to explain her behavior. The word *nephew* is one of many relational or familial concepts and images used during the Gulf War. This word signals the operation of a complex semiotic system. Here I want to indicate only how the media, wittingly and unwittingly, influenced the structure and meanings of the messages sent about the yellow ribbon through a complex and comprehensive cueing campaign.

Other segments of society also participate in the cueing process. The Washington officials who controlled the placement of monuments in that city are a case in point. Recall that Maya Lin's memorial was a source of controversy leading to the commission of the Hart memorial. The most recent and complete representation of the combined forefronting of the image and the ideology of American romance is the Women's Vietnam Memorial.

Before examining this instance of mediation, however, I shall turn briefly to the cinema's recovery role in the mediation of white male pain. The cinema has had a major collusive role in using the romance motif of white pain. The 1990s hit movie *Forrest Gump* is perhaps the most notable illustration of this form of collusion.

Recovery Cinema Mediates White Pain: The Case of Forrest Gump

> *The sap is rising in America, and his name is Forrest Gump. . . . In this country, there's nothing harder to argue with than success, and to nearly everyone's surprise, Forrest Gump, has become a success . . . but few things need to be challenged more fiercely than this gentle, defiantly peculiar account of an idiot's pilgrim's progress through decades of American country.*

> *Stiff as a pole with his hair cut military short and his shirt buttoned up Adam's apple, Forrest Gump has become the pop-culture hero of the 90s. He's emerged as an Everyman symbol of all things to all people, moving from movie reviews to the op-ed pages, where essayists and critics have compared him to everyone from Huck Finn to "Harvey's" Elwood P. Dowd.*
> (Hal Hinson, The Washington Post 1994: G 1,1)

Students of ritualism have found that rituals that facilitate "nonbloody" conflict resolutions often build on disruption and conflict (Beers 1992; Nieberg 1973; Werbner 1989). In pursuing *Forrest Gump* as a mediation of white pain, I propose a parallel argument: both explicit constructions in the movie itself and the resulting public discourse are part of the white mediation of the pain associated with the radical 1960s. That is, not only is white recovery encoded as a preferred racist/sexist narrative in the movie, but also the audience, reviewer, and critic may help concretize the preferred understanding, despite the possibility of diverse audience receptions and readings.

Since the early 1970s there has been an upsurge of "gendered conflict" in popular movies (Hedley 1994) and racialization of violence in the cinema (Giroux 1995). I have called this rhetorical strategy a "rhetorical reversal" (Gresson 1995). Because it helps clarify the cultural work of films such as *Forrest Gump*, let me briefly define and illustrate the rhetorical reversal before proceeding further with my analysis of this film.

Reversal is a pivotal tactic with a most interesting logic. It pertains to the power to name, define, and negotiate reality. In the 1960s, Blacks engaged in such behavior around the notion of "Black." Before the 1960s, this word held largely negative connotation for most American Blacks, but by seizing and embracing the word "Black" and investing it with positive value, Blacks engaged in a most significant form of reversal. One of the major reflections of the power shift, at least, symbolically redefined meanings according to their own interests. It is, for instance, now a part of Black folklore that Quame Toure (Stokely Carmichael) told the white press, "Black Power means whatever we say it means."

Blacks have assumed a different oppositional style in recent decades, focusing increasingly upon elaborating the nature and liberational role of Black literary and cultural theory and criticism. Instead, white women have increasingly assumed the vanguard challenge of white male appropriational tactics. The struggle for "self" control has been essential to this challenge of the canon. For example, "making reversals" is a major feminist strategy. (Gresson 1995)

Five interrelated dynamics seem closely associated with rhetorical reversal:

1. the experience of a personally debilitating loss of one's share in a collective hegemony, whether deserved or not;
2. a public—first personal, then collective—effort to recover the pragmatic and moral losses;
3. a gradual convergence of the public and private actions and analyses;
4. their dual justification and legitimation by various factions within society through negation of the previously reigning rhetorical situation; and
5. the gradual emergence of a reconciliatory, more inclusive formative image, purged of the former negativity of the lost moral context.

Both the oppressor and oppressed may participate in this recovery rhetoric tactic; thus, either out-group members or members of the oppressed group may direct reversals at the oppressed. The relative differences in history and real differences in power, however, ultimately make such rhetorical arguments less than persuasive.

In *Forrest Gump* we see it the rhetorical reversal reach new heights of pedagogic destructiveness as it reteaches a generation the old ideas of racial positionality and distorts the history of mid-twentieth-century cultural politics. A film review in the *Detroit News & Free Press* (February 18, 1995: C7) describes the movie thus:

> The film views the social tumult of the 60s and 70s through the innocent eyes of Forrest, a slow lad who nevertheless understands right from wrong and leads a charmed life. Forrest . . . falls in love with Jenny, a beautiful girl who decides to pursue a worldly life of hippie protesting, unbridled sex and drug addiction.

Their morals and behavior have different consequences. Forrest becomes a sports star, survives the Vietnam War unscathed and becomes a rich
entrepreneur. Jenny wanders away from an abusive home to an abusive
Berkeley boyfriend to prostitution, eventually contracting AIDS. . . .

Few things are that straightforward, however, and the review continues:

What *Pulp Fiction* and *Forrest Gump* represent is an Academy Awards contest
between conflicting views of art. *Pulp* is the modern notion that art must
shock and attack, which become ends in themselves. *Gump* returns to the
idea that real art rediscovers virtuous truths that inspire people to do the
right thing.
    The public has already cast its ballot for *Gump*, but we will have to wait
until March 27 to see if the academy feels likewise.

By constructing Forrest Gump as an innocent white male, one with less
than normal intelligence, the mythmakers have found a means of mediating white pain. The white man who has no idea of evil, no active or conscious intent to hurt "others," cannot be held accountable for the way
things happen. If racism, natural disasters, and sexism abound, so be it. In
the midst of these horrible natural and man-made events, there remains a
white man wholly innocent, wholly vulnerable, wholly open to the world
and its contingencies. Movies like *Pulp Fiction* and *Forrest Gump* reject the
portrayal of the United States as racist, sexist, and classist, and both rely
on a shared narrative of American redemption and regeneration through
violence (Slotkin 1973). Henry Giroux summarized the implications of
movies, notably *Pulp Fiction*, that racialize violence:

Instead of focusing on how larger social injustices and failed policies, especially those at the root of America's system of inequality, contribute to a culture of violence that is a tragedy for all youth, the dominant media transformed the growing incidence of youth violence into a focus on
black-on-black fratricide. . . . Such racially coded discourse serves to mobi-
lize white fears and legitimize "drastic measures" in social policy in the name
of crime reform. . . . Moreover, the discourse of race and violence provides a
sense of social distance and moral privilege that places dominant white society outside of the web of violence and social responsibility. (1995: 333–34)

By neglecting this dimension of the racialized discourse of both *Pulp
Fiction* and *Forrest Gump*, the aforesaid review juxtaposes false opposites
and suggests that the decision to be made by the awards committee is
somehow apocalyptic, a decision for either good or evil. In this way, the
review participates in the white recovery project, for it suggests that

Gump—both the movie and the character—stands on a moral high ground that abrogates its share in the misrepresentation of reality.

Related to this misreading is another, that the public is a monolithic whole consciously determining the inherent moral value and worth of a cinematic creation by its vote at the box office. And yet there is something to be learned from the tone and turn of this review: the critics themselves are part of the fuel propelling the recovery project forward. This is so because of the way the critics responded to *Gump*: its transparency invites a critique that will itself become an opportunity for critique. Consider, for example, Hinson's criticism of the film:

> The strange thing here is that people who normally consider themselves too sophisticated for such a banal "feel good" message are being suckered by the picture's savvy packaging and swallowing it whole. They don't seem to notice—or don't care—that Gump doesn't direct his life in the way that most characters do and has no real motives or drives or psychology. When Gump asks Jenny to marry him, declaring, "I'm not a smart man, but I know what love is," they're happy to believe him even though there's nothing in the movie to suggest his statement. (1994: G1)

I agree with Hinson here, but I question whether we are ever that sophisticated, especially in regard to cherished values and redemptive ritualization. During this phase, resistance is little expected or tolerated, and those who do resist are eventually punished by whatever means available. Hinson's comments state the "truth," and yet it is precisely this "truth" that, once uttered, becomes neutralized again and again as movie critics gloss the "truth." This "truth," in the eyes of an increasingly cynical public, becomes more evidence of "political correctness gone amok."

Instead of yielding to this murderous ideological frenzy of the left, radicals, and minorities, "reasonable" people see the world through the eyes of Gump. This applies even to astute critics. Gene Siskel, for instance, explained:

> Our Flick of the Week is *Forrest Gump*, which begins as yet another case of a Hollywood star doing an Oscar turn playing a mentally disturbed character (Charly, Rain Man) but surprisingly turns into a marvelous, whimsical epic of contemporary America. That's because Forrest Gump (Tom Hanks) is more vehicle than person in this film, a vehicle that drives us through the last 40 years of American history. (July 8, 1994: B4)

Recognizing that Forrest is a vehicle does not seem to alert Siskel to ask what precisely Hanks is a vehicle for: what's the tenor? The emphasis on "whiteness" (and "blackness") in the first several minutes of the movies goes unexamined. Siskel is not alone, however, in his oblivion to the racial recovery encoded in the story. Thus Peter Travis, of *Rolling Stone*, says:

> *Forrest Gump* is a movie heartbreaker of oddball wit and startling grace. There's talk of another Oscar for Tom Hanks, who is unforgettable as the sweet-natured, shabbily treated simpleton of the title. The Academy is a sucker for honoring afflicted heroes. In Hollywood, it's always raining rain men. . . .
>
> Zemeckis [author/director of the film] doesn't fall into the trap of using Forrest as an arrested development. He knows the limits of a holy fool who can't understand the hypocrisy of postwar America that this picaresque epic so powerfully reveals. The peace-love pretensions of the 60s are skewed as neatly as the greed decades that follow. But there is something of Forrest that Zemeckis would like to see rub off on us: his capacity for hope. It's an ambitious goal in this age of rampant cynicism. Godspeed. (Travers 1994: 99)

Film reviews like these invite us to participate in a sacred ritual in which the complexity and pain of the past several decades are cast off for an optimism that can obtain only if we participate in collective denial or, to use Russell Jacoby's term (1975), "social amnesia." *Amnesia* is a good term to introduce here because it traditionally has pertained to a psychological stratagem used by the mind to defend itself from painful memory or awareness. What many people have understood regarding America since the early 1970s is that it seems intent on forgetting: first Vietnam, then the liberation struggles of the 1960s, then the folly of using wars like the Gulf War to conceal economic recession and the pathos of late capitalism. Nonetheless, it has been equally as clear to many that just as the amnesiac cannot be forced back into awareness, some forces in American society resist honest self-examination and self-accusation.

One mechanism for managing this "loss of memory" is the rhetorical reversal (Gresson 1995). One of its most powerful expressions has been the attack against "political correctness." By insisting that efforts to regulate immoral, unjust, and destructive beliefs and behaviors are themselves flawed and by encoding this stance as a righteous campaign against "political correctness," a diversity of actors have come forth as a "Give-Me-a Break" bloc. This pluralistic power bloc, heterogeneous in many ways, nonetheless shares the belief that being corrected can become a bore and irritant. It is against this backdrop that the more critical film reviews may be read as assisting the recovery project, for this project is aided most often by situated support than that grounded in compliance with a comprehensive ideology. When applied to the case of negative film criticism of *Forrest Gump*, we can see the silencing power of the rhetorical reversal as "anti-PC" discourse. For example, given such a discursive climate, the following criticism, while cogent, seems both uninformed and anticlimactic:

> Now Forrest is hardly the first idiot hero to ride through a fiction, bodies dropping all around him. . . . Gump, however, refuses to suggest its idiot might be mistaken—he must come out a winner. . . . And America is cheering. Much as it cheered Ronald Reagan, who, . . . is the real proto-Gump. Reagan too was relentlessly upbeat. Reagan too was extraordinarily lucky. And his luck, like Gump's, was often built on the backs of people who suffered off-screen. Forrest had bankrupt shrimpers, martyred Vietnam buddies, and his wife, whose death was remarkably demure, considering her ailment. Reagan scored points off America's poor; somehow managed to cloak himself in heroism while apologizing for a needless screw-up that killed 241 U.S. servicemen in Beirut; and avoided tarnishing his reputation for optimism by spending too much time on AIDS. (Van Biema 1994: 82)

Nor did several others seem to find a listening ear:

> I can't see how people with low I.Q.s or those who love them are in anyway comforted by all this hogwash. I can easily see how such people might be offended by its smug unreality. (Kaufmann 1994: 28–89)

> This movie is so insistently heartwarming that it chilled me to the marrow. There are no moral crosswinds here, not a breath of doubt or unease to ruffle the Gump image . . . at once mazy and tight-assed, it foists upon us the myth that we can know better, and do better, by being dumb. (*New Yorker* 1994: 79)

Michael Apple (1993), among others, has pointed to the failure of liberal and left critics to understand the sensibilities of the contemporary public. These reviews seem to bear him out, and their tone of moral righteousness is precisely the quality the right employs in turning the public against the left: "Don't Ram It Down Our Throats!"

Yet another leftist theme prompts even greater reactionary disdain. Consider the acidly cogent review by Amy Taubin:

> As you might have expected, I'm grumpy about *Gump*. This is, after all, *The Village Voice*. Like Kilroy before us, we were there at all those zeitgeist moments so we can tell for a fact that Forrest was not. . . . I can't write off the historical revisionism as an F/X spoof. The sight of Forrest picking up after that nice Negro girl on the steps of the University of Alabama pissed me off

as much as Gene Hackman and William Dafoe's *Mississippi Burning*. White men: the past, present, and future are forever yours. (1994: 53)

This allusion to "white men" works largely to convert the converted on each side. Likewise, in *Time*, Richard Corliss astutely pegged the film as a "male weepie," noting that "the only three movies of the past two decades to win both year's box-office crown and the Oscar for Best Picture— Rocky, Kramer vs. Kramer, and Rain Man—were canny, poignant fables of men in domestic crisis" (1994: 52–54).

These movies were about "white men," not just men, and the "domestic" crisis was less about domination by the females in their lives than the recovery of white male positionality in the popular imagination. These movies, like *Forrest Gump*, are a kind of romance—that is, they point to an idealized desire: the longing for something just beyond the immediate grasp, the concrete given. In each instance, a white man is re-united with his "before the fall" condition; and women and minorities are enlisted in the recovery. To see how the movie, *Forrest Gump*, joins the Yellow Ribbon ritual as a media ritual, we need only scratch the racial/sexual surface of the celluloid representation of an America that never was.

Gender, Race, and Romance in Forrest Gump

From my reading, Gump—like many contemporary Americans—understands only what he wants to understand with respect to race matters. With the black female earlier and Bubba's momma later, he silences their implicit representations of racial reality by not recognizing racial moment or tension. The scriptwriters operate through other vehicles as well. The audience, for example, is asked to recall the stereotypical Aunt Jemima as a remnant of the racist past in the "nonracist" present. Moreover, they try to deepen the image of Forrest as "racially pure" by fusing him with Bubba in front of the lieutenant, who is clearly elitist and implicitly "politically incorrect," if not racist, because he makes fun of Bubba's lips. Of course, it can be argued that many people seeing *Gump* have no racial memory of the allusions to blacks having thick lips, but this then raises the question of inclusion: why, then, refer to his lips as a site of humor or interest?

Race is not the only site used to re-inscribe an innocent white maleness. Consider Gump's female love object. Jeannie is "guilty" of more than just promiscuity and ignoring Forrest's Vincentian devotion. She also is a coward, telling him as he leaves for Vietnam: "If you are ever in trouble, don't try to be brave, just run away." Presumably, this advice is intended to show her love for him and to recall that she was always telling him to run away from the bullies as a child. But her comments, given the failure to develop her character, mutes these nicer representations by emphasizing the idea that she, unlike Gump, has never grown up and recovered from the trauma of a painful childhood. Reviewers, too, struggled with the gender themes in *Gump*:

He's a simple do-gooder with an I.Q. of 75 who lives by his doddering mama's (Sally Field) philosophy: "Life is a box of chocolates; you never know what you're gonna get." During the turbulent 1960s and 1970s, he worships his mixed-up childhood confidante (Robin Wright as an abused waif who samples all the antisocial vices of the time) while he himself becomes a college football star, a decorated Vietnam hero; a Ping-Pong champ; and a business tycoon. (Williamson 1994: 40)

Although there has been some discussion of this dynamic in the feminist literature, few traditionally mainstream accounts take up the issue. Yet as is notably the case with *Forrest Gump*, Hollywood has been moving for some time toward disenchantment with the female or, as the reviewers call it, the passing of Hollywood's "Year of the Woman": "Forrest Gump's mother is so devoted to him that she sleeps with the local school principal to guarantee her son's 'mainstreaming.' Forrest's best friend Jenny is a similarly diminished woman . . . [although she finally] . . . bears a healthy and bright son and conveniently dies" (Ottenhoff 1994: 860).

It is at this point in my analysis of *Forrest Gump* that we can perhaps best see how its dynamic unfolding fuses or converges with aspects of the yellow ribbon ritualism surrounding Vietnam. Many students do not agree with this interpretation, and I don't insist that they do. But I do insist on considering alternative readings and not accepting that the academy and classroom are neutral sites transmitting neutral information and inviting "independent" thought and action. Interestingly, the relative impact of this alternative pedagogical effort can be seen in the response that this reading elicited in one graduate education student.

Paul H. was a twenty-eight-year-old white male completing his master's degree in education. He was married to a Mexican American woman and had one child. In addition, he had served in the navy and taught in the Southwest. He planned on returning there when he had completed his work in math education. It was clear that his background and experiences significantly influenced his willingness to consider and explore the recovery perspective I had shared with his class.

After returning from a visit to Washington, D.C., to see the various war memorials, he brought me several photographs he had taken. He had seen in our discussions of *Forrest Gump* a linkage to the Women's Vietnam Memorial. What I had tried to help the class see was the way that gender is used to close in on and mediate the societal tensions emerging from multiculturalism and diversity enhancement activities. I had argued that the movie reflected a common feminist critique: The periodic need to reinscribe the patriarchy's dominance over females and other minorities requires that a particular imagery and ideology be forefronted. Paul H. saw the memorial as a possible illustration of this view. After further exploration I discovered the memorial has a characteristic pose, what I have designated the *Pietà Embrace*. I use this designation after Michelangelo's *Pietà* (ca. 1500) and the ideology of American romance. In the conclusion, I examine more fully this aspect of the interplay of gender, class, and recovery in the mediation of white male pain.

Conclusion

The most recent and complete representation of the combined forefronting of the image and the ideology of American romance is the Women's Vietnam Memorial. This memorial, dedicated in 1993, shows three military nurses—a white, a black, and a Latino/Indian/Asian—mourning the death of a white male soldier. The white male soldier is held by the white female nurse as the black nurse looks heavenward and the Latino/Indian/Asian nurse kneels on the ground gazing at the soldier's helmet. This memorial is used as the cover illustration for *America's Atonement*.

What a powerful memorial, but whatever its merits, this compromise monument is an unmistakable departure from the original concept, as Elizabeth M. Norman explains:

> In 1984, two former army nurses from Minnesota and Wisconsin proposed a monument honoring women who served in Vietnam. They founded the Vietnam Women's Memorial Project. The prototype statue, which they hope will eventually stand in Washington, D.C., is a woman dressed in combat fatigues; she has a stethoscope around her neck and bandage scissors sticking out of a pocket. (1990: 135)

This reworking of the public memory of Vietnam and its problematic status—especially among women who opposed the war as mothers and mates—is yet another instance of the recovery process and suggests still another way in which the relearning of race can be contested. Cultural

studies have taught us the value of narrative: stories are critical to establishing subjectivity and, by the operation of empathy and remembrance,
believability. Stories are rhetorically powerful tools. *Forrest Gump* illustrates this and more. When his friend Bubba dies, Gump tells us: "Bubba
was my best good friend, and even I know that ain't something you can
find right round the corner. . . . Bubba was gonna be a shrimping boat cap-
tain, instead he died right by that river in Vietnam."

How can you not love Forrest? I also lost black brothers in Vietnam,
and I recall that they were drafted into war in numbers greater than their
presence in the general population and that they have been perennially
defamed and exploited by a harsh homeland. I like Forrest's story, but I am
offended by the men and women who stand behind his alleged idiocy.
They have him perform complex and profound social acts, eliciting in the
process the compassion and complicity of those without a cultural memory of the contexts defining the events so nicely grafted onto the persona
of Forrest Gump.

The racially coded recovery embedded in the ideology of romance
serves to sever the white male persona from the rest of society—whether
Kevin Costner in *Field of Dreams*; Mel Gibson in *Lethal Weapon*; Bruce
Willis in *Die Hard*; Sean Connery in *Just Cause, Medicine Man*, and *Rising
Star*; Patrick Swayze in *Ghost* and *To Wong Fu with Love*; or Tom Hanks in
Forrest Gump—and having so severed him, excludes him from complicity
in—and responsibility for—the social upheavals and crises characterizing
the cultural landscape.

The call back to whiteness encoded in these various movies must be
understood as such, and the corruption of public mourning and compassion at the service of reactionary and undemocratic policies of contain-
ment must be recognized and challenged. By understanding "whiteness"
as a curriculum and pedagogy, we move toward de-essentializing racist or
sexist behavior by holding accountable the agents of racist schooling, including the media.

The portrayal of the Vietnam War in public schools (Kincheloe and
Staley 1983) was a powerful illustration of the nature of American patriotism and its intrusion into the curriculum and pedagogy of education.
Moreover, Susan Jeffords (1989) argued that the continued popularity of
Vietnam-related courses in the college curriculum pointed to the complex
cultural work done by the representations of Vietnam as cultural product.
In this chapter, I examined three interrelated ideas: gender, redemption
impulses, and recovery representations. The gender issue has been the
overriding concern.

A major concern of education reformers in the past several decades has been the exposure and elimination of practices that perpetuate unnecessary and unfair differences between males and females. One of the findings of the research on bias in the classroom is that female teachers who feel themselves above gender discrimination may also practice sex bias against females, those belonging to both minority and majority groups. For some people, this raises the question of how women can be taught to carry out practices that undermine women's liberation. Tania Modleski put the problem in this way: "We need to consider the extent to which male power is actually consolidated through cycles of crisis and resolution, whereby men ultimately deal with the threat of female power by incorporating it" (1991: 7).

For Modleski, women's activism on the behalf of gender equity threatens male domination in ways that lead men to undermine their efforts. Much research supports her argument (Daly 1978; Jeffords 1989; Melosh 1989; Roszak and Roszak 1968). One way this has been achieved is by getting women to turn their attention to taking care of or nurturing the men in their lives: husbands, fathers, sons, brothers. This tendency has been so effective and thorough in a society centered on the patriarchy that even oppressed groups parallel this model. For example, the late Audre Lorde characterized the necessity of black female self-love as due to an overcommitment to the oppressed black family: "In the light of what Black women sacrifice for their children and their men, this [call for self-compassion and self-love] is . . . much needed" (1979: 18). Rhetaugh Thomas Dumas echoed her when she wrote: "I have felt the pangs of guilt evoked by those who would lead me to believe that to protect myself and promote my general welfare is to let my people down" (1980: 214). Mediating white pain is not a simple task, nor is it unimportant or overstated. The resurgence of racism, especially on our college campuses (see *Baltimore Afro-American*, April 27–May 3, 2002), reminds us that critical work remains to be done in those places where whites feel threatened by others culturally, politically, or economically. We must be mindful of the need for and the methods of mediation. The mediators, moreover, often are women and assume salutary forms. Thus the primary Web site addressing the Women's Vietnam Memorial reported:

> Glenna Goodacre discovered the heart of a nation in the process of creating the Vietnam Women's Memorial. Seldom does an artist have the opportunity to be involved in an artwork that means so much to so many people. As Goodacre says, "To think my hands can shape the clay that heals the heart." She's rightly proud of a work that makes visible a memory while shaping the perception of that memory for future generations.

These words, by Susan Hallsten McGarry, are true. But they expose more than truth; they expose motive and mediation. We recognize in Goodacre's efforts precisely the kind of culture work Mary Daly argued that women pursue at the behest of the mythmakers. Thus, in confronting the lack of critical analysis that Kincheloe and Staley decried in 1983, we must again focus on the subjective value of certain actions beyond the question of "truth seeking" or "doing the right thing." Certainly, one persistent point implied in Gramsci's discourse on hegemony is the convergence of needs and interests between the dominators and the dominated.

It is often here that the mediation of pain finds both a vehicle and a tenor for production. In the next chapter, I explore the mediation process as it is expressed in the biographies and narratives of prospective teachers. I also address the new discourse confronting democratic, critical pedagogy: nonoppressive education for those not sanguine to a radical discourse and pedagogy.

A Postscript: The Second Gulf War

The specter of Vietnam has been buried forever in the desert sands of the Arabian peninsula.
PRESIDENT GEORGE BUSH, 1991

This week the United States and its "coalition of the willing"—England, Australia, and Poland—invaded Iraq. Thus began the formal war to liberate Iraq from its leader, Saddam Hussein. The outcome of that war has yet to be determined despite the American declaration that the outcome—total victory—is all but achieved. History may reveal many sidebars to this war. One is already evident: the American media is "embedded" in the war zone and, at times, seems complicit with the Bush Administration. The media has skirted the question of biased involvement, but not completely. Peter Arnett, the veteran reporter for NBC and National Geographic, exposed this fine line reporters walk when he granted an interview to Iraqi television and expressed his belief that the United States had failed to achieve some of its objectives in the war. Many NBC reporters grieved for him even as they distanced themselves from the disgraced, disowned, and temporarily unemployed journalist.

There are other *mediation* tensions evident among the media covering the war and world opinions regarding the United States' ideal self-image. On one occasion, a MSNBC correspondent in Turkey held a live, focus group with several Turks. This audience made it clear that they disliked

Saddam but they did not think much of the United States either. Puzzled and flustered, the reporter asked, rhetorically, how could a non-Arab, secular state hate us? The very question reminds one of the themes taken up in this chapter regarding the American self image as honest, decent, democratic, noble savior of the free world.

At the conclusion of the session, the reporter observed what non-American media had been saying all along: people outside of the United States do not see the linkages between September 11, 2001, and the pain it caused our nation as the basis for what is happening in Iraq. The reporter also observed that viewers ought to be concerned that what we see on television differs dramatically from what is seen in the rest of the world.

This chapter began with a reflection: America is unwilling to examine its policies and practices. We have an image problem. This image problem is complex. This is not so much because America, like most nations, has both noble and ignoble interests. Rather, it is because we claim to stand above the rest—in the eyes of God and Man. Yet issues such as ruthless corporate capitalism, racism, and the like continue to plague the nation. For example, the first female casualty in the Iraqi war was a Native American mother. Her presence in Iraq on behalf of an oppressed people is uncanny given the continuing plight of Native Americans in this country.

Contradictions like this are part of the reason that the U.S. "trails in the battle for world opinion" (*The Atlanta Journal Constitution* Sunday, March 30, 2003, www. ajc.com.) and has to wage a "war for hearts and minds" (Kurtz 2003; Roberts 2003). The confluence of domestic and international racial practices is illustrative. In particular, the perception that the United States has invaded a "colored nation" fuses with the recognition that blacks, for instance, are less favorable toward the war than whites. An article (*The New York Times*, Thursday, March 27, 2003: B15) on New Yorkers' war views, by Randy Kennedy and Diane Cardwell, is illustrative. Citing a recent poll where only thirty-four percent of blacks supported President Bush's presidency, these writers quote a black nurse:

> "It's like Muhammad Ali said," she explained. "He said: 'Why should I fight? The Vietcong never did nothing to me.' Well, the Iraqis never did anything to me or mine. Why should we fight?"

The sense that the war in Iraq rehearses the Vietnam conflict is suggestive. It is also suggestive, but yet to be discussed, that the only "fragging" incident in the current war involves a black noncom who threw grenades into his superiors' tent, killing two and wounding more than a dozen officers (see "Grenade attack a fragging?" *Sunday Telegraph*, 23 Mar 2003, www.dailytelegraph.news.com). How we mediate these and related events have great significance for the future character of our nation.

Today we see that we still refuse to examine our foreign policy or the contradictions embedded in our ideologies of "American decency" and "democratic leadership" of humanity. We refuse to see what millions of others see when they look at us—the most powerful nation in the world, a country that has little need to feel vulnerable to others since the fall of Russia. We also refuse to see ourselves as arrogant in our power. The rising tide of "Arab anger" expressed in the media confuses us because of this refusal. We seek to "understand" the "Arab mind" even as we reject knowledge about our own mind.

The profound significance of this refusal is concealed in the words of the elder Bush after the first war in the Gulf region in 1991. Bush, mindful of the cultural crisis Vietnam constituted (Rowe and Berg 1991), echoes the sentiments of those unwilling to learn from America's duplicity. Instead, we use war to "bury" our sins. Today, we blanch at the mistrust ordinary Iraqis have toward America's declaration that this time we will go all the way: having seemingly removed Saddam Hussein, we will make Iraq a democracy in America's eyes. It is because of this contradiction in our values, needs, and practices that we seek to manage what our own people see.

The 2003 war in post-Saddam Iraq continues this style of crisis management. The embedding of the media helps manage the pain. Americans have been fed an almost surrealist set of war themes on MSNBC, FOX, and CNN. The future will decide how the world comes to view this practice in the scheme of things. Whatever that judgment we know that George W. Bush's chagrin toward the "nonpatriotic" and critical questions raised by the Press corps reflects the very weakness Kincheloe and Staley observed in 1983. Today, decades after the yellow ribbons and antiwar rallies characterizing the Vietnam era, we again see yellow ribbons— and antiwar rallies—everywhere. And both pro- and anti-war proponents chant the one sincere mantra: "We support our troops!"

·4·

WHITE PAIN AND THE SEARCH FOR A POST-OPPRESSIVE PEDAGOGY

I teach this course in women's studies. I have about seventy students, all white except for one black female. There are about twenty white males in the class, and it has been going really great until today. We were discussing "white privilege" and the white males took over. One declared that blacks are the privileged ones; he said that "black privilege" is the Negro College Fund. Another white male agreed, adding that the fact that he cannot freely walk through North Philadelphia is also "black privilege." All of the women seemed scared to challenge them.

Prologue

A short time back a former student called me for a consultation. After polite conversation, she began softly weeping. Eventually, after drying her eyes with tissues I had given her, she explained her tears in this way: "I'm sorry; I just had an unbelievable experience with racism." My first thought was that she had encountered an angry minority person striking out at a vulnerable white woman. But she quickly explained the reason for her distress with the words opening this essay. A semester earlier, this woman had taken my graduate course on critical theory, gender, race, and representation. Despite doing well in that course, she told me that she now felt ill equipped to help her students and hoped that I might be able to suggest something that would help her convince them that the Negro College Fund and North Philadelphia were not truly instances of "black privilege."

The challenge faced by this young educator is a formidable one. We have already seen some of the barriers to introducing a democratic and critical pedagogy to those personally unfamiliar with the pervasive social oppressions in our society. In addition, the notion of white pain has alerted us to the potential assault implicit in an anti-oppressive agenda. In this chapter, I focus on recent efforts to forward the social justice initiative within education while respecting the presence of white pain and the rights of those who may not readily identify with anti-oppressive perspectives and strategies. I thereby extend the earlier discussion of white pain in the academy by exploring its presence in the multiculturalism classroom. I begin with a brief statement of the assumptions giving rise to what came to be known as "multicultural teacher education."

The Rise and the Fall of Multiculturalism

During the decades leading up to the twentieth century, a powerful struggle was underway to both define and defend the dominant ideas of who was American and what was his (not "her") rightful inheritance. Concepts such as "manifest destiny," the "Negro problem," the "Yellow Peril," "killing the Indian and making the man," the "woman problem," and "manly Christianity" were just a few of the ideas signaling an effort to convert many eyes into one vision and rigidify the established pecking order (Bederman 1995). World War I and the New Deal Era (which encompassed the Great Depression) stand as important events symbolizing, if not inviting, a silencing of the multicultural backgrounds and diverse interests among Americans (Melosh 1991). War and economic and political ferment seemed to legitimize the suppression of difference and the insistence on universal suffrage. A myth—"the melting pot"—was the ideology used to explain this suppression of difference in life experiences and choices.

With the upsurge of the 1960s radicalism, these earlier tensions regarding race, gender, ethnicity, class, and sexuality regained national visibility and threatened the myth of a melting pot society with a multicultural mandate. The insistence on a more equitable share in the American dream by those traditionally excluded resulted in a plethora of movements. Ideas such as the "War on Poverty" and the "Great Society" professed a "vision of possibility," a conviction that the United States was truly a participatory democracy and that the "scarce resources" of the richest nation on earth would be redistributed more equitably. The social changes and political discourse associated with black liberation or civil rights activity gradually widened to cover a wide range of real and perceived oppression of students, women, the young, the elderly, gays, and the physically handicapped.

This may be viewed as the rise of multiculturalism as a perspective or orientation. The idea of multicultural education grew out of this larger social context. Lois Weiner, for example, writes that multicultural teacher education took shape as African American educational issues were enlarged to include a diversity of minority groups:

> This growing concern that nonwhite, nonnative speakers of English were being educationally shortchanged enlarged the category of disadvantaged students. The *Thesaurus of* Eric *Descriptors* introduced the term *multicultural education* in 1979, defining it as "education involving two or more ethnic groups and designed to help participants clarify their own ethnic identity and appreciate that of others, reduce prejudice and stereotyping, and promote cultural pluralism and equal participation."
>
> This orientation stood in stark contrast to the acculturation rhetoric that held all Americans were blended into a "melting pot" and thereby indistinguishable from all others in essential ways. Because of the threat this newer understanding held for many, the term "identity politics" came to signal the conflictive or combative aspects of an orientation that discredited the truth or value of a monolithic "American identity." (1993: 38–39)

Writing from a minority-sensitive perspective, Louise White reflects the typical understanding of the challenge of multiculturalism for prospective teachers. Because teachers' attitudes, beliefs, and behaviors are typically shaped by their own environments, their impact on student achievement is through an

> unconscious reflex rooted in the teacher's own middle class background combined with training which consciously or unconsciously may not recognize the possibility of alternative cultural styles and cognitive modes. This combination results in a middle American ethnocentricism which is destructive to minority students, students from poor families, and any other student who deviates from the mythical norm espoused in teacher training institutions. (1973: 309)

Lois Weiner viewed the 1970s as the era of competency-based teacher education (CBTE) and multicultural teacher education, two strategies to improve teacher preparation for urban, minority education:

> A report issued jointly by two committees of AACTE, one on multicultural education, the other on CBTE, outlined their agreements. Teachers "need certain unique competencies in order to teach in culturally diverse situations," the editor noted. Another writer explained that "for most Blacks, bad teaching . . . is most often less a matter of a teacher's deficit in commonly

practiced teaching skills than a matter of the reflection of a teacher's fundamentally negative feelings or expectations for Black children." Multicultural CBTE focused on the attitudes teachers needed, as opposed to cognitive
skills, since the teacher's primary role was defined as the "facilitator of the
acquisition of value systems consonant with a student's ethnic, cultural and
linguistic background." (1993: 49)

The tremendous social demands for greater social justice for minorities
and participation in the mainstream resulted in notions like "diversity"
and "inclusion." Future generations of teachers also found as a part of
their "inheritance" the expectation that they would be "multiculturalists."
This expectation has persisted even as the social and political climate has
recycled to the "right" with a corresponding shift in the dominant discourse of social justice. It is in this newer discourse that the emergence of
white pain is most apparent. It is also within this discourse that multiculturalism has been characterized as a potential oppressor and serves as an
impetus for an alternative ideological stance: the pursuit of social justice
through an anti-oppressive educational strategy.

White Pain and the "New" Anti-Oppression Discourse

Some years ago, the late Donald Willower, my mentor and colleague,
gently chided me for insisting that race remained a major factor in society
and education. He had been drawn to and influenced by the writings of
the black conservative sociologist William Julius Wilson, author of the
important book *The Declining Significance of Race* (1980). Wilson had
gained prominence, but not without considerable debate and critique (see
Gresson 1982), for promoting the thesis that history and class, rather than
race, accounted for the continuing societal inequities between whites and
blacks in America. For Willower, this idea was persuasive, perhaps because it allowed us to continue working toward change without directly
confronting racial or other non-class-based explanations for oppression
and social inequality. Willower's preference to view and address our
problems without confronting racism is perhaps visionary. There is considerable evidence that we are increasingly pursuing nonracial configura-
tions of certain social injustices with correspondingly nonracist solutions
and strategies for change. This newer orientation, broadly concerned
with democratic education, emphasizes education for social justice
(Darling-Hammond et al. 2002; Dilg 1999). Part of the importance of
this emerging discussion is its insight into the pedagogy and psychology
of healing. This can be seen in a recent debate facilitated by the American

Educational Research Association anti-oppression in education (Butin 2002; Kumashiro 2001, 2002).

The first essay was published in 2001 by Kevin K. Kumashiro, in which he argued for the pedagogical usefulness of the "posts" perspectives, that is, poststructualism, postmodernism, and postcolonialism. Perhaps the main contribution of this piece was its presence in *Educational Researcher*, for it eased the way for other scholars to share their own understandings of this somewhat marginalized or radical academic perspective. Dan W. Butin was one of the scholars who responded to Kumashiro. Butin (2002) understood Kumashiro's arguments on behalf of the "posts" perspectives as useful but problematic. His goal was to expose their limits and indicate how the perspective of Michel Foucault (1977, 1978) might overcome the danger of oppressing classroom learning and growth. Butin succinctly stated his central concern thus:

> The problem is that resistance has been conceptualized as something done only by those oppressed and oppression as something done only by educational practices antithetical to anti-oppressive education. While Kumashiro acknowledges that anti-oppressive education may be "emotionally upsetting" (p. 8) and that we may actually "desire teaching and learning in ways that affirm . . . the silencing of other possible worlds" (p. 5), there is no discussion of the possibility that anti-oppressive education may itself be a pedagogy of silencing which is resisted by those in disagreement. . . . we must acknowledge that anti-oppressive education imposes itself upon students, from the texts to be read to the intellectual positions defended and attacked.
>
> . . . anti-oppressive pedagogy does not admit the possibility that it too makes use of power in order to reject particular perspectives. I suggest that a "posts" perspective can. And in this admission lies a reformulation of teaching that provides an opportunity to fashion a less constrictive classroom practice. (Butin 2002: 15)

Kumashiro, responding to Butin's essay in a companion reflection, chose a very "post" and powerful strategy: "As I read and reread Butin's commentary, I found myself attending to different aspects of the commentary and responding in different ways, depending on the lenses I used to read" (2002: 17).

But the strategy of multiple readings did not conceal the heart of Kumashiro's concern with Butin's apparent "resistance" to understanding what the "posts" perspective on power could yield:

> There are several problems with this argument. "Posts" perspectives do not make it possible to say that a practice or perspective is "clearly" or "truly"

anti-oppressive since they insist that all practices and perspectives are partial. . . . When reading Butin's commentary a second time, I felt concerned and found myself wanting to illuminate and problematize Butin's resistance to anti-oppressive education. Butin's discussion of an example from his own teaching experiences exemplifies the certainty and resignation that is commonplace among educators and that often hinder anti-oppressive change. . . . As an alternative, Butin argues that pedagogies informed by "posts" perspectives "construct situations within which students come to their own understanding of the issue in question," regardless of whether that understanding is something the teachers consider "oppressive" or not. (Kumashiro 2002: 18)

Kumashiro highlights the notion of *resignation* but rushes on to cite Butin's other offenses. Kumashiro has correctly stated the value of "posts" terms such as "disruption," "resistance," and "tentativeness." His motive for a multiple reading, however, rehearses the very flaw in Butin that he exposes. He seems to know that one cannot continue to sit on the fence, or more precisely, that the insistence that one not "contaminate" science, including educational theory and pedagogy, is bogus. This very insistence is itself ideological and "contaminated." Thus his allusion to "resignation."

There is a strategic loss, or resignation, that can accompany the failure to see that even democracy and "nonintrusion" (often called "interference") cannot be privileged by those who are struggling under the yoke of oppression. Discourse situated in the academy—vaguely insulated against the devastation of ruthless power—can afford to discuss matters under the rubric of "reason." People living under the oppressive yoke of a particular brand of democracy may not be able to grant its "greatness" above all else. The Iraqis suffering Coalition bombing in Baghdad come to mind in this regard: Are we truly liberating or only killing them?

Kumashiro's arguments on behalf of the "posts" perspective triggers something akin to the response against "whiteness" studies: white pain and white retreat. Why? Butin illustrates the critical point: "Yet to presume that we can simply change to become less oppressive is to presume that our 'old' perspectives are just wrong and denies the contextual nature of how we come to believe what we do" (2002: 15).

Butin is trying to construct a classroom space, complete with possibilities and potentialities, that will "quicken" students' inner workings, yielding a "free thinker" who can do what she or he will. His conclusion is seductive if not persuasive:

I hope that other classes, other situations, may further disabuse them of perspectives I deem objectionable. But this is irrelevant to my particular project. My project is to construct situations within which students come to their own understanding of the issue in question. Their understanding may be in direct opposition to my own perspective. Their understanding may be labeled oppressive. But that is the price I pay for conducting a "posts" classroom. Advocates of anti-oppressive education may balk at these suggestions. And well they should, for they offer only haphazard control over what the student will learn. But a pedagogy grounded on a "weak overcoming" is exactly one that embraces the partiality and unknowability of the teaching process. Constructing situations that force students to confront, resist, and resignify their identities and knowledges is what makes teaching an art form. One cannot know the end result, but I am not so sure that attempting to control it is a road better taken. (Butin 2002: 16)

This takes us back to power and power relations and to what has already been constructed in the mainstream pedagogy and curricula: oppression. Kumashiro offers important corrections to specific points made by Butin, but his forcefulness seems muted in the face of what has been charged:

By implication, a pedagogy informed by "posts" perspectives does not hope that students embrace or come closer to "the" anti-oppressive practice or perspective, nor does such a pedagogy need to resign itself to the fact that students might instead embrace oppressive ones. Rather, it hopes that students question the effects of a variety of practices and perspectives, including the ones their teachers say are anti-oppressive. In particular, it teaches students to look beyond a variety of practices and perspectives, not to reject what they are taught, but to examine and experience ways that any practice or perspective can produce different knowledge, identities, relations, and so forth, sometimes oppressive ones, sometimes anti-oppressive ones, and sometimes both. (Kumashiro 2002: 18)

Together, Butin and Kumashiro provide a vital service. They expose the complex challenges, indicating the limits and possibilities of the classroom teacher if certain logics of theory, policy, and practice predominate. They also highlight the implicit challenges of a psychopedagogy of healing that is responsive to white pain. But their analyses neglect one important dimension of this healing: the minority-based lessons of anti-oppressive education.

Anti-Oppressive Education—A Minority Perspective

Minority teachers in the classroom offer a critical alternative vision of anti-oppressive education. Butin and Kumashiro do not directly confront this dimension. In particular, white males typically receive much more deference and submissive student responses than women and minorities do (Schacht 2000). While a white male may be rejected or resisted for presenting multiperspectival material, it seems to be minorities and women who most often find themselves challenged by, and challenging for, students who might resist anti-oppressive material. The conversation about "posts" perspectives lacks any recognition of these gender-, class-, and race-specific dynamics. This exclusion pertains most to the possibility of a detached exchange and construction of multiple learning sites. Indeed, I maintain that the very presence of a minority authority figure typically and routinely stimulates potentiality and possibility in challenging ways for most students, regardless of their background demographics. Let me illustrate.

Between April 13 and 23, 1993, a web-based discussion of male alienation in women's studies classes was held on WMST-L. A few excerpts provide a sense of the complexity mere attention to minority content may introduce:

> I have recently been approached by one of my students complaining that my course focuses entirely too much on women's issues. The course I am teaching is an Introductory Criminal Justice course. In the course description I mentioned that the focus of the course would be to critique the criminal justice system especially in respect to gender and racial discrimination. I also mentioned on the first day of class that I would be teaching from a feminist perspective. This student argued that he is not getting the "basics" he needs for law school. The text book . . . covers the basics and is not from a feminist stance. This confrontation was very upsetting to me. I started questioning my teaching style only to discover that I have not focused on women's issues any more or less than racial issues and other extensions of the "basics." As I began talking to faculty I discovered that many professors who try to teach from a more inclusive perspective are attacked by their students—either directly, as I was, or through teacher course evaluations. I am relatively new to this list, so I don't know if this issue has been raised before, but I was wondering if anyone else has had similar experiences, and if anyone has suggestions about ways to teach from an inclusive perspective without alienating students—especially white males. Thanks (AGAIN!).

This writer was a female professor at Notre Dame. Her story stimulated dozens of e-mail replies. One male response to her plea adds an interesting, perhaps predictable, dimension.

> My question for you is: have you quantified just how much time you spend on women's issues? I would guess that this student is perceiving a little as a lot. I have had similar experiences in teaching Introductory Statistics. In

that class I have used word problems for including diversity. When I ask students to comment on the word problems there are always some who say "most of the problems deal with women's issues" or "too many deal with homosexual issues". In fact, a content analysis of the 300 word problems I use in a semester showed that about 1 in 6 deal with gender issues and less than 1% deal with sexual orientation.

I think that one of the problems we will always face in including marginalized groups is the false perception that a little inclusion is a lot. Notice the phenomenon of last fall's elections. That was dubbed by the media the year of the woman. Yet when all is over there are still only 6% females within our U.S. Senate. While this may be a 3 fold increase it is still hardly more than a beginning.

This male respondent offered a powerful insight into the plight of the pro democratic educator. But one may intuit a certain resignation in his comments, which rehearse that found in the Butin-Kumashiro debate. Another male seems to echo the concern I am raising:

. . . You've hit a very important nerve with your observation that being inclusive is seen by some as being narrow. One student commented on my evaluation that I am too pro-women. I considered this a victory, not a criticism. What pleased me is that the student did not say I was anti-men. I take pains to be fair and inclusive. I allow no gender bashing in my classes. Since men and women are accustomed to having knowledge presented in the "neutral" male voice, they perceive the inclusion of women's voices as being a special interest and not the basics.

The challenge presented by "sensitivity to white males" and others who might resist anti-oppressive education is shown to be massive in these excerpts. Interestingly, the insights of multicultural educators are seen as helpful in healing the divide. Hence another respondent wrote:

This is in reply to Patty O'Donnell's query about alienating male students in classes. I don't have any real answers to the question, but I would call everyone's attention to Patricia Williams' book *The Alchemy of Race and Rights*. In it, Williams describes many scenarios exactly like the one she described. Maybe it helps just to know it isn't you as the teacher that's the problem. What makes it even more relevant to Patty's situation is that Williams is a lawyer teaching in a law school. You might think about using it in the class; at least you might want to read it.

African Americans like Patricia Williams have, understandably, been at the forefront of sharing narratives of the unprecedented tensions created by their authority positions in the white academy. A major concern for myself and others has been the initial, ironic silence that white students frequently display, regardless of the content or position assumed by the minority educator. Gloria Ladson-Billings writes, "Student silence can be many things, but for those who are truly interested in pedagogy (particularly a pedagogy of difference), student silence can be deafening. It should not, however, be ignored" (1996: 85).

Ladson-Billings echoes and enlarges the sensitivity and insight minority educators and other democratic-oriented teachers bring to the multicultural classroom. Britzman and Pitt expand on the silence management theme she introduced:

> In our work, we learn from listening differently to the responses of our students, resisting our own impulse to self-mastery that seems to require us to view the students as in need of our correction. This orientation, we now believe, is the teacher educator's rush to application. Learning to listen to the structures that students display delays our own mastery. We do not know what will happen, but a great deal of our work concerns returning the student's question back to the student. The returned question has nothing to do with pleasing the teacher but, instead, may provide . . . more space for the student to consider her or his own conflicts in learning. (1996: 123)

By allowing "more space" for students to grapple with "resistance," multicultural educators reflect awareness of the painful nature of much learning and growth; they recognize the need to "dwell in" the teachable moment with their students. It is this "dwelling in," as the phenomenologist describes it, which serves as a bridge-support for the neophyte seeking to push beyond the safe borders of self-other understanding.

The commitment to anti-oppressive education, we see, has not suffered from a paucity of committed, non-oppressive teachers. Indeed, the liberatory ideas discussed by Kumashiro and Butin have been advanced by many earlier writers, including Ann Berlak:

> Changing, for members of dominant and subordinate groups who have internalized dominant stories, might not only mean coming to read experiences from the perspective of the oppressed. It may be possible to construct new stories that incorporate both (or several) stories into a single narrative where complementary versions that had previously been told and heard in isolation from one another are constructed into a single story in which the different versions match up. We would then be part of one another's stories—I would be part of your story as you are part of mine. Such stories would be tales of the painful effects of racisms that are, though to different

degrees, experienced by all racial/ethnic groups, by both targets and perpetrators of racisms in Eurocentric and racist societies. Such stories, likely to
be unfamiliar to both White peoples and peoples of color, would include
narratives of White supremacy, but they would also frame racisms as community shared traumas that result in blindness, alienation, and deracination
for us all. (1996: 100)

Implicit in Berlak's storytelling strategy is the notion of "shared fate"
(Kirk 1964). First introduced in the mixed racial adoption studies of H.
David Kirk, this concept refers to his observation that the more successful
adoptive parents tended to be those who could acknowledge both their
adoptive children's and their own "difference" rather than deny that either
the child or they were defined partly by the adoptive condition. I have
used the term more broadly to describe any condition where two or more
people identify a sharedness (1995). Berlak's partial solution to the implicit oppressiveness of anti-oppressive education reflects this condition
between the oppressor and the oppressed.[1]

The multicultural educators introduced in this section seem to share a
common belief in the need for catharsis and the value of storytelling in the
anti-oppressive classroom. Although storytelling does not address the full
range of challenges facing democratic education in the non-oppressive
classroom, it does introduce the opportunity for student growth in a less
threatening environment. It also represents a step back from the insistence of guilt with respect to student participation in social oppression
(read as oppressive monoculturalism). Further, it builds on accepted
understandings of constructivism as a compelling description of the role
of subjective reality in the processing and possible internalization of new
information. In the next section, I describe my own effort to introduce
storytelling and autobiography into the emotional work characterizing
much anti-oppressive education.

Emotion Work in Multicultural Teacher Education

At SUNY-Albany, I taught cross-cultural clinical practice and family therapy techniques to working- and middle-class white females. At Penn
State, my profession changed but my students are similar. Over the years,
I have observed that much of the thinking characterizing a "liberal pedagogy" failed to deal with the existential realities of these students and the
constructivist nature of the multicultural classroom. As a result, I have developed and implemented a series of courses that incorporate constructi-

vist insights. I have been especially interested in how students understand their social positions and how they construct their narrative selves and relate them to the multiculturalism mission. Several ideas presented in the preceding sections underpin my curricular strategy. In addition, the approach I take has been informed by particular attention to the pedagogic implications of "social pain" and autobiographical work in the multicultural classroom. I turn now to a brief elaboration of this concept and how I have implemented it in my work.

Social Pain, Student Subjectivity, and Anti-Oppressive Education

Social pain is pain—psychical, physical, spiritual—caused by social beliefs, values, or actions. It derives its meaning from society because most pain is ultimately mediated or understood through ideas, beliefs, and meanings that humans collectively construct. As I have defined it, racial pain is an aspect of social pain; likewise, white pain is a variant of racial pain. Multiculturalism as pedagogy "invites" specific "pain zones" for many white students. Some of the pain stimulated is inevitably linked to being "healthy." Audrey Thompson, writing on psychologically oriented whiteness theories, clarifies this point as follows:

> For psychological theorists of whiteness, a healthy white racial identity will not become possible until whites confront and accept their whiteness (abandoning colorblindness), acknowledge the privileges of whiteness, and take a consistently antiracist stance. The keys to developing a healthy white identity, then, are (1) developing an *awareness* of whiteness, including white privilege; and (2) acting in ways that make use of that knowledge to challenge personal and institutional racism. (1999: 2)

Pain is generally recognized as either healthy or unhealthy. As a signal to some incipient or latent danger, it is healthy; but as the signal of advanced disease, it is considered unhealthy. The questioning, resisting utterances of white students regarding multiculturalism issues and projects are, in this view, healthy. I suggested earlier that a certain degree of pain and loss are inevitable in a truly multicultural teacher education curriculum. Denial of this necessity is itself illustrative of the inevitable social pain (racial, gender, class) that accompanies growth. For example, black middle-class teachers in urban schools have been often observed to be ineffective with lower-class, urban black pupils (Anyon 1995; Yeo 1995). For them, as for white teachers, often important social structural and institutional factors underlay their failures (Shujaa 1996; Weiner 1993). Relational factors emanating from these societal dimensions also are experienced at the individual level. Denial of individual responsibility or contemporary liability for presumably past (and therefore not currently operational) oppression fails to help in working beyond social pain. The efforts of multicultural teacher educators to track the stages or dimensions of these reactions to a transformative pedagogy may, accordingly, be translated as therapeutic actions or "social therapy."

The idea of social therapy has its roots in those areas of psychological treatment that appreciate the importance of connecting some forms of individually experienced social pain to the cultural or systems dimension of human functioning (Bowen 1985; Lyman 1981; Spindler and Spindler 1994). Some correctives to white pain may be achieved by linking critical pedagogical ideas and therapeutic strategies. By critical pedagogical ideas, I mean largely instructional strategies aimed at transformation. By linking the "therapeutic" to critical pedagogy, I forefront loss, pain, and the healing implicit in a critical multiculturalism. But there is one sense in which anti-oppressive pedagogy may indeed be vulnerable to its characterization as oppressive: the assumption of "taintedness" by oppression may preclude the presence of "victory" over oppressive practices, or at the least, an openness to the gradual awakening to the inevitable presence of oppressive proclivities in us all. The so-called constructivist perspective in education has provided a partial corrective to this assumptive arrogance in its emphasis on the subjective role in the construction of knowledge and the understanding of new information. According to Ava McCall in her discussion of constructivist implications for teacher education:

> In order to heed Liston and Zeichner's advice to teacher educators to balance introducing social reconstructionist ideas to students with addressing their concerns as preservice teachers, we must know students better. We need to learn more about students' backgrounds and interests as well as develop a greater understanding of what contributes to their acceptance and resistance to feminist pedagogy and multicultural, social reconstructionist ideas. Even though the time needed to accomplish these goals might be significant, these efforts could become research studies and teaching improvement projects. (1994: 65)

It is perhaps ironic that the multicultural classroom could sometimes be less than democratic and less than edifying, especially when we consider how much thought and energy most multicultural teacher educators give to curriculum and instructional matters (Bollin and Finkel 1995; Darling-Hammond et al. 2002). Still, we need to remind ourselves of the importance of engaging "students' experiences as central to teaching and learning. This means that teacher educators need to accept that the learner is an active participant in the construction of knowledge" (Karpol and Brady 1997: 11).

The recognition of student teacher constructions in the classroom is a critical yet too seldom emphasized challenge, especially with respect to multiculturalism. Realizing with Wortham and others the value of what I call *cognitive-emotional distance* from the material, in my classes I assign a term essay that allows for both autobiographical reflection and critique. An article by Linda Valli (1995) facilitates this initiative. In her article, Valli reports on a study of nine white preservice teachers placed in predominantly black urban, multicultural schools. Her intention had been to give these prospective teachers an experiential learning opportunity. I assign this article for two reasons. First, Valli's task or intervention engages the cognitive-affective domains of student teacher multicultural experience and thinking in a way that allows my students to more or less safely enter the discourse. Second, Valli provides one of the most sensitive and accessible discussions of certain contradictions in multicultural teacher education. Reflecting on the two contradictions with which her students repeatedly struggled in their multicultural education ("learning to be color blind" and "color conscious"), she advises:

> How can this analysis guide teacher educators in helping preservice students construct cross-cultural identities? The first and most obvious way is to show the limitations of the two mandates. The first reinforces stereotypes; the second imposes cultural domination. Only when they are viewed in dialectical relation do the mandates reveal the tensions and issues of race that new teachers must learn to handle. (Valli 1995: 126)

In this formulation, Valli has made accessible for further intervention the contradictions of teacher education identified in earlier work, notably that of Mark Ginsburg (1988). Reporting on teacher education research at the University of Houston, Ginsburg identified many of the problematic aspects of prospective teacher beliefs cited by other scholars. As a partial corrective, he calls for the development of a "critical praxis" among prospective teachers. I have found his work provocative and especially valuable for graduate students. Undergraduates, however, often have difficulty seeing themselves in terms of these contradictions, as Bollin and Finkel (1995) report. Because of the way in which she conducted and describes her work, Valli seems to resonate better with my undergraduates, as they see themselves in her student teachers. A brief presentation of excerpts from several of their reflective essays may help illustrate the pedagogic value of subjective classroom exercises in the multicultural student teacher classroom.

Student Autobiography and Non-Alienated Pedagogy

To date, I have more than a thousand student reflections on Valli's work as it relates to their own student narratives. The results have been largely remarkable. Perhaps the most immediate value of the article as a pedagogical tool is to give students a chance to introduce themselves as "heterogeneous whites" with complex multicultural genealogies. Consider the following statement made by one of my students in his term essay/reflection on multiculturalism:

> Though I was not raised in a very diverse environment, the times that I grew up in, and the role models that I had, gave me a strong awareness and appreciation for the different ethnic groups that make up the larger world. I grew up in the State College area. My father was a professor of Philosophy and my mother was from an affluent Boston family. My mother's background help shape my perceptions of society with its enlightened Unitarian heritage.

This is an important comment. It not only invites whites to recall a history of liberal thinking and acting, but it also identifies contemporaries as situated in terms of the past. Without a vehicle for challenging the contradictions inherited by many students, this kind of sharing might have been truncated or silenced. While it is true that few of my students enter the class with this specific genealogy or pedigree, each enters with her or his own story and understanding regarding her or his diversity in the world. To challenge problematic positions is one thing, but first they must be heard. Already in the preceding passage, we recognize a "family memory" that often is underexamined in the multicultural classroom discourse: the perennial presence of "good white folk" even during times of "dirty racial business."

The young man just cited links his multiculturalist vision to a specific and unique biographical inheritance: "Her [his mother's] great, great grandfather, Charles Loring Brace was the founder of the Children's Aid Society in New York City, and a boyhood friend of Frederick Law Olmsted, whose *Cotton Kingdom* (1861) was one of the mainstays of the abolitionist movement." Clearly, this could be read as yet another instance of a student giving the professor what he wants to hear. Recall this is precisely what one of my critics (chapter 2) claimed my students were doing. But consider this: the student too may have an investment in seeing him or herself in a certain way. In fact, a major objective of anti-oppressive education is to allow "space" for enlargement of self-identity and self-ideal. The kind of student storytelling implicit in Berlak and others cited previously creates precisely this opportunity to change/construct biography.

This particular instance of a recollection of past glory actually exposes the dialectical nature of all knowledge construction; moreover, it illustrates recent understandings of the growth challenge to "whiteness":

> Rearticulating whiteness is an emergent project. We know the racism of our whiteness in part through recourse to particular methods of inquiry but in part also by our own resistances to change and by our temptations to see ourselves in particular racialized terms. A temptation for progressive whites is to not only be a good white but to be *recognized* as a good white. Identifying oneself as an anti-racist ally or aspiring to a final stage of moral white development, however, evades the problematic character of whiteness. In a racist society, whiteness is an inherently problematic position. (Thompson 1999: 23)

Audrey Thompson has gone to the heart of the matter: there is a need to see oneself and be seen by others as "a good white person." Ultimately, for those committed to social justice, this need is critical if social pain is to be avoided. Beyond the offense against democracy implied in the notion of oppressive anti-oppressive education is another: the offense against an emerging self, one potentially moving toward enlargement. Interestingly, this very theme surfaces in the reflection of an African American male with a strong Afro-centric orientation, who uses the occasion to critique teacher educators generally:

> The problem . . . is that courses in which undergraduate education majors are prescribed—vestiges of one of our most recent revolutions in programs pertinent to the process of training future teachers—have not fulfilled the hope of bringing prospective teachers sociologically intimate to the growing minority-dominant society. Closer to the point, these courses were established in the wake of this country's drive toward multiculturalism, even cultural pluralism, yet, as the author concedes, it is widely believed that they have failed to sensitize students. In fact social stereotypes that were prevalent throughout her early upbringing—generalizations that members of her generation fought somewhat heartedly—are considered to be on the rise amongst generation x'ers. My concern is that teacher educators are engaging in multicultural efforts with little knowledge of beginning teachers'

experiences in culturally diverse schools. Often, teachers try to incorporate multiculturalism into their curriculum without any knowledge of it themselves, which only leads to the encouragement of stereotypical attitudes and generalizations. Although multicultural education is a necessity in all classrooms today, if it is not incorporated appropriately, it could backfire and instead do more harm than good.

These thoughts remind us of the negativity that might accompany multicultural educational activity. What I have recognized from years of teaching cross-cultural, often emotional, material is the fact that I, a black male authority figure, create tension for my white students. I often mention this to them when explaining how minority students might feel with white teachers. For them, my presence becomes a source of "white identity crisis." I have referred previously (1997) to the task necessitated by this white identity crisis in multicultural education as "emotion work." What exactly is this pedagogical challenge? Perhaps one way of thinking about it is through review of an inquiry by Stanton Wortham (1994). Using techniques from linguistic anthropology, Wortham examined how something as simple as a classroom discussion using "participant examples" can affect one's teaching objectives:

> Discussion of an example sometimes leads classroom conversation off track. In such a case speakers do not get back to the topic that led them into the example. Instead, they move out from the example into a new topic—often inspired by the example. . . . Although the speakers may be overtly talking about the example, their characterizations of participants in the example can have implications for these same participants in the classroom conversation itself. When these implications become salient, the example can lead the classroom discussion off track. (1994: 1–2)

In this passage, Wortham's argument is reminiscent of earlier inquiry into the linguistic features of classroom material (see Haskell 1987). But Wortham's inquiry extends the focus of earlier work in this area; in particular, he documents the progression of classroom interactions that, starting from a seemingly neutral position, degenerate into extraclassroom partisanship. It is here that we see the special significance of his findings for multicultural education: its skepticism of the efficacy of participant examples that promote extended classroom interaction.

Writing around the time of the applied research reports of several multicultural educators (see Bollin and Finkel 1995; Valli 1995), Wortham concludes in regard to "enacted participation": "If a teacher wanted students to experience certain interactional events and emotions . . . a participant example might help, if it encouraged student to lose control in the classroom interaction. But then the class would have to *step back* from this experience and reflect on it in light of the text" (1994: 171).

These last thoughts are important, as they speak to both the constructed nature of the curriculum and traditional classroom practice. In addition, they alert us to the undeniably deconstructionist character of radical curricula that insist that students confront the inherited or "official knowledge" (Spring 1995). Furthermore, Wortham implicitly reminds us that we cannot escape the interplay of cognitive and affective content in certain kinds of pedagogical activity. Therefore, while his inquiry does not pertain precisely to multicultural education and discourse, it may be extrapolated to them in terms that may help us better understand some of the "backlash" themes identified in recent scholarship (Apple 1993; Dziech 1995).

Implicit in my African-American student's critique, supplemented by Wortham's work, is the issue addressed briefly earlier: the threat multicultural inclusion per se constitutes in the classroom. For example, an Asian American student noted:

> Regardless of whether or not a teacher has moved beyond the color of a student, it is oftentimes impossible to make other students see their classmate for who they are and not for what race they represent. For example, I feel that in all of my classes, when any issue about Asians is the topic of discussion, most white students turn to look at me. To them, I represent my whole race and I am knowledgeable about everything that is Asian. Needless to say, this is far from the truth, yet I find that I am often in this position.

This student uses Valli's findings to talk about her classmates. As characteristic of most of my Asian students, she rarely spoke in class, although she performed well otherwise. Indeed, only once in thirty years have I had an Asian student challenge directly her white peers about whiteness and its privileges. I make this point not to imply something "essential" about Asian Americans; rather, I want to indicate how an observed tendency seems to be modified through autobiography when used as a nonthreatening invitation. Few whites or minorities are likely to have the background and perspective needed to succeed in multicultural situations. For most people, a complex developmental process is involved in gaining the maturity, competence, and other qualities associated with a transformative, multicultural challenge. But some do seem to recognize the hurdles. For example, consider a young man who is currently completing his student teaching in South Dakota at an American Indian school. In his paper, he wrote:

A lot of students who become student teachers haven't for the most part, encountered any relations with inner city black students or inner-city kids of all races. This situation would put a student teacher in a threatening situation, at least from their point of view. This would most likely be the case because they never were exposed to black students or the environment they live in. Case in point, in my Art Education class this semester, I posed a question to my peers; "how many of you in this class would go into an inner-city school and teach?" One person out of twenty-four students raised their hand. I then asked why they wouldn't want to teach in an inner-city school. Their replies were, "I'd be afraid," "there is too much violence," and "the kids are too mean."

This young man is twenty-eight years old, born and raised in Pittsburgh. He has three older brothers and one younger sister. He writes admiringly of his hardworking parents, of German, Irish, and Italian background:

My parents both had to drop out of school before finishing high school. My father dropped out in the tenth grade to go and work for the family and tend to his mother. My mother dropped out of school in the ninth grade and her reasoning was because of her mother being ill. Both my mom and dad came from low-income situations. My dad's father was in the U.S. Army and his mother stayed home and took care of the three children. My mother's dad, well I am not to sure of, I don't know what he did or his background. He died when my mom was only five years old. Because of this my mother doesn't remember much of him. Her mother took care of her and her two brothers. My parents both had very rough childhoods but seemed to come off it OK.

My father worked two jobs his entire life. My mother didn't start working until 1982. By that time all of the children were in school. My mother also worked two jobs and still does. My parents were and still are hard workers. They never had much for themselves because everything went to taking care of the five children and never had extra money for themselves. This was the main reason why our family didn't take many vacations. . . . My father passed away in May 1992 of a heart attack, he was forty-eight years old.

This story is familiar to many working-class white and minority families. I make this possibly challengeable point because Mike seems "very black" to me. In my vernacular community, this term means that he has the sensitivity from both knowing pain and interpreting it in a broad-based way that leaves his racial identity intact without withdrawing or escaping into the meager white privilege that accrues to whites for promoting their racial group. In short, Mike has that form of whiteness that constitutes the positive side of whiteness found in the writings that I have recently designated as the "recovery school of white studies" (Gresson 2000: xi).

Mike's narrative is remarkably different from those offered by most of my white students. To be sure, they write about family trials, tribulations, and triumphs, and even about family values and honor. But few reveal intimacy with the raw brutalities of living near the "class line." Most of us are prepared to see a different picture of "whiteness." Another male, Todd, illustrates this:

In second grade I won the citizenship award that my elementary school gave to the most outstanding citizen in each grade. I guess it actually meant the one who didn't get into trouble and the one who was generally nice to others. I guess that is what a citizen of our country is supposed to do and I certainly wanted to please my country. My parents were both at the assembly and I was so proud of myself. I guess that I have never lost that feeling.

I was born in a centennial year of all coincidences and I was raised a good old American boy. I played baseball, sang in the Methodist church choir, and always watched fireworks on the fourth of July. I had no real sense of my family origins and I still don't. I know that my father's great grandparents were from Scotland and my mother descends from England, but this was far from important to me and, from what I could determine, to my family as well. As far as I know, I am solely an American and the rest of it doesn't much matter.

My family was constructed as the model U.S. family. My parents raised their three children together in a middle-class suburb where we played in the backyard and walked to school. My father worked in a management position and my mother stayed home to take care of us kids. I can't remember a time when I didn't have almost everything that I wanted and I always had food on the table. I rarely think of myself as ever identifying with any ethnic group, although I guess that is not completely true. The most powerful portion of my identity that would define my ethnicity would have to be my religion. This played the biggest role in defining my values also. I was forced to go to church every Sunday along with Sunday school and the church choir. There were and are almost no ethnic minorities that attend my church. Yet I obtained Christian values from the church that strive towards equality for all, forgiveness of all and salvation for all that believe in Jesus and it is this set of beliefs with which I identify most.

This passage emphasizes the values that students often bring to the multicultural classroom. These values serve as cueing lenses, helping students simultaneously recognize and assimilate new, potentially damaging, information. Narratives like the preceding remind us of the contrast between these privileged lives and those of the vast majority of the minorities they will learn about in multicultural classrooms. Both privileged and poor whites, notably males, face a challenge in such classrooms. There is evidence, nonetheless, of transcendence among some of them. Transcendence requires, however, a reason and a vehicle for change within. Mike, introduced earlier, had gone into the military, served in Alaska, and known many lonely months during which he could think about life and his place in it. He once shared some of his journals written during this time in Alaska. A dominant theme was the painful sacrifices of his parents, notably his father who suffered and died during his absence from the mainland. Mike's encounter with multiculturalism was drastically different from that of most of his peers. As a result, his reflections often seemed elitist or superior with respect to his typically younger classmates:

> I am a junior here at Penn State and I have seen the bias and stereotypes that take place and play themselves out. Being from the inner-city of Pittsburgh, I can see the so-called "bad side" of what teachers perceive to be a bad thing in the inner-city schools (e.g. violence, drugs, fights, etc.). This is a false accusation. The inner city is no worse off than any suburban school. I am convinced that the problem isn't just black people, it is with teachers not knowing how to deal with or communicate with the students. In my opinion, this goes beyond race; it is ignorance and selfishness on behalf of the educator. Until educators understand how to deal with multicultural issues, they will be fighting the notion of racism and stereotyping until the day they either quit or retire.

Mike later married a middle-class woman whom he says marveled at his background and take on life. After he finished at Penn State, he acted on his multicultural understanding and commitment. He and his wife went to South Dakota to teach at a Native American school. Thus differences in background can affect both understanding and optimism. For example, listen to Jennifer:

> I am a white American female with strong beliefs that have been taught to me by my elders. My family origin is from Germany and Wales; however, I do not feel a close bond to these two countries. I have a very tight affiliation with the country I have known all my life, America. My loyalty to my country will assure that I will be the best teacher I can be to the future of our nation. Being from the city (Philadelphia), I have had a first-class look at some of the things that affect the children of the inner-city. Although I went to a suburban school, my dream is to educate children from the urban areas. These children are faced with horrific ordeals and settings. For instance, chains and bars on windows, unqualified staff, etc. I know that my parents

raised someone with outstanding values that can help to "save" these children. I would not be happy teaching anywhere else but the city. I have alot [*sic*] to give. Although I am a white American, I want to teach African Americans. This may be because my father, who was superintendent and president of the PA School Board Association, has always told me "I can make a difference and I will."

Looking ahead to two years from now when I will be looking to start my career as a high school educator, I can't help but think back to the third grade. I have many memories of coming home after school and retiring to the basement to teach my stuffed animals on my small green chalkboard. I even remember begging my mother to bring home a grade book and a plan book so I could "officially enroll" all of my stuffed animals. My father, an intermediate school business teacher, and my mother, the intermediate school ninth-grade secretary, would come home every night and always discuss the latest school gossip at the dinner table. I guess I was conditioned to be an educator from the very start.

The key thing I want to emphasize here beyond the obvious influence of biography is the tone or quality of concern expressed by those students who do choose to face the social inequities of the multiculturalism mandate. Their voices are faint compared with those who choose the "safe" way; yet their voices are powerful because of the very privilege they enjoy. According to Angel, a junior,

My future plans consist of student teaching in a Philadelphia inner city school, spending the next few years teaching disadvantaged children, and eventually holding a powerful position in society where I can improve education for those children. . . .

In elementary and junior high school our family was quite poor, though I never really [knew] this at the time. Later in life our family would change our social-economic status to upper-middle class. This has proven to be a critical point in my life as I have seen first hand how one is treated just on the basis of their apparent status. . . . I must quickly explain to you that I lived in Pennsylvania the first four years of elementary school. Here I was among all white students, but I was poor. Immediately I was placed in a remedial reading class, hence considered inferior. Then, in 4th grade, I moved to Florida where my school was half minorities and half white. After my experience of feeling less valued as other students in Penn, now in Florida I was privileged and saw others suffer because of my fortune. Coming from where I came did I know this was wrong and could really empathize with minorities. I now wonder if I would have felt the same that I did if I had never seen that other side. What a scary world we live in. In these schools tracking was based on anything but ability. It was all a game, masterfully devised to keep the top on top and the bottom on bottom. What was considered an asset was having money, prestige and being white. I remember sitting in classrooms and knowing that what was happening to the students in the class wasn't fair. I think that was the first time I was ashamed of being white. If I misbehaved it was acceptable. If my work wasn't right it was re-examined. For some reason those teachers thought I was better than minorities. I was privileged.

All of these experiences that have made my life what it is, have pushed me to become a seeker of justice, I decided to take my mother's advice and begin where a lot of professional instructors turn away—the inner-city. Where else is the fight for justice more important than in the lives of our children—our future? My influences have provided me with the right tools to be the kind of educator disadvantaged children need on their side. Everyone deserves a fair chance in life and I have the resources to help win that fight.

The understandings of these youth about themselves and others are both inspiring and instructive. In an earlier discussion, I challenged the idea of some of my critics that students are saying only what I want to hear, and I will not repeat my rebuttals. But I do want to restate my faith in the personal and professional integrity of these young people. I further believe that the so-called posts perspectives can be taught proactively yet nonoppressively.

Conclusion: Toward a Pedagogy of Transformative Mourning

Yesterday in my minorities and education class, several students led a discussion of Asian American experiences in the United States. I was particularly struck by one woman who shared her experience of emotional distress at learning about the horrible things done to Chinese Americans and Japanese Americans over the past hundred years. Because her presentation dealt with instructional aspects of teaching to or about Asian Americans, she was concerned with how to tell young white children about the Asian American past. She felt that children should not learn about this past because even she had had a hard time with the information; but she recognized that failure to teach it was part of the perpetuation of the injustice toward Asian Americans. Several class members joined in with recollections of the absence of any information about Asian Americans at various points in their education. A few noted that they were about to graduate and still had not learned about these things in social studies education and methods.

I was gratified that these students had researched the topic and that the class had been able to do some "emotion work" around it. Before this class—and with only three weeks left in the term—I had become more than a little despondent. Weekly, I watched the class of sixty struggling through the various presentations, anxiously awaiting the Thanksgiving break, and passing their enforced attendance at these presentations with "mental trips": reading the student newspaper, doing crossword puzzles, quietly chatting, and "sleepin'-in-class." But on this day, they came alive; they could understand the dialectical tension I so often reminded them that they had inherited. Something about this particular classmate's emotionality hit home. Their eyes largely conveyed "lights on; somebody's home," and I felt the students' engagement when I connected the class discussion of perceptions of Asian Americans to the current furor in Decatur, Illinois, and Cairo, Egypt. In Decatur, there was concern with Jesse Jackson's presence and advocacy on behalf of six black students that received two-year suspensions from a white school administration for fighting. In Cairo, officials and citizens were fearful that Americans would blame the entire nation if it were learned that a single Egyptian pilot was criminally responsible for the fatal airplane crash last week.

The sense of this student that her own "white pain" regarding Asian Americans cautioned her regarding the propriety of teaching this information to young children reminds us of the dual task we face in multicultural teacher education. We are trying to reach future generations by "reteaching" the current generation. This is the ethical challenge we face. I personally experience it as more than a matter of ethics. For me, like the heroine in Tennessee Williams's *A Streetcar Named Desire*, I have long "counted on the kindness of strangers." I may or may not have the "professional license" to tell students about my racial vulnerability, my racial autobiography, or the like, since this fails to carry the "imprimatur" or "*nihil obstat*" of the academy's Magisterium (the "teaching church" operating out of the Vatican in Rome). But I have a commitment to black children and families who must also count on the kindness and justice of "good white folk" if we are to continue winning the battle against "evil" however understood.

I make clear to my students that their primary task is self-growth, self-enlargement. I can tell them this because I am, at fifty-six, a part of the past that they study, a part of the "wretched other" that they seek to help, to deliver. And yet as a trained academic with two Ph.D.s, I belong to the "cognitive elite" that Murray and Hernnstein (Gresson 1996a) celebrate; thus I am "qualified" to "teach" in the academy even with my "marginalized" logic of inquiry. I tell them "my truth," having already defined it as a part of the dialectical inheritance they endure. What is this truth? What is important for them as prospective teachers is to gain some critical perspective through relating their own inherited strengths and social understanding to the multicultural condition.

When Max Rafferty denied the possibility of a future for multiculturalism, he certainly could not foresee a time when whites would feel alienated in places they had created and control. Still, the racial pain expressed by Rafferty seems similar to that expressed by the two young men convinced that certain organizations—the Negro College Fund—and geographical regions—North Philadelphia—are "black privilege." Because they constitute the dominant social grouping, their words and actions often conceal their underlying pain. For some, it may seem like an unnecessary waste of time and energy to dwell on the nature of and solution to this form of pain. After all, because whites continue to dominate the United States and much of the "civilized" world, it might be legitimately asked if they need "liberation fighters," especially minorities, to be their advocates.

I believe the answer to this query is yes and no. Along with a number of other scholars, activists, and humanists (Giroux 1997; Ipsaro 1997; Winant 1997), I believe that contemporary whites occupy a unique historical position. Extrapolating from W. E. B. Du Bois's concept of "double consciousness," Howard Winant (1997) calls this "white dualism." I have previously viewed this social context and historical space as a transitional one in which emotional life is largely characterized by efforts to hold oneself together with ideas and beliefs—I call these "self-other metaphors"—that help one feel whole (1987, 1995). As it pertains to whites, this condition often leads them to feel like victims of a confused and brutal society. This quality, or "schizophrenic" tendency, is evident in the preceding illustrations. It also is pervasive in American society. Yet perhaps nowhere is it more evident than in the academy: universities, schools, and other learning-specific enterprises and institutions. It is in the academy that we see the battleground in microcosm: whites in pain, carrying on a symbolic and substantive war against the fictional enemy, diversity and affirmative action. In the final chapter, I take a closer look as some of the themes and tensions attending the pursuit of racial healing.

·5·

—

TOWARD A PSYCHOPEDAGOGY
OF HEALING

Mourning and Mending Difference
in the New Millennium

*Those people [white South Africans] have the capacity of destroying this
land. . . . If there were not the possibility of amnesty, then the option of a
military upheaval is a very real one.*
BISHOP DESMOND TUTU (ROSENBERG 1997: 86)

Prologue: An Ability to Mourn, a Key to Healing

Some years back I spent a wonderful weekend with a white South African couple and a close friend. The friend had just returned from South Africa where she had been the guest of this middle-aged, upper-class couple who run a psychology institute in one of the major cities. They had come to South Carolina as her guests. For me, this couple was a welcome relief from a painful encounter I had had many years earlier, in 1972, while on tour in Europe with several other white South Africans. I found this couple not only very decent and racially sensitive but also anxious to communicate to me the tremendous racial changes taking place in South Africa. The only difficult part of the visit was the pain I felt at their sense of historical guilt for the evils of apartheid and their current ambivalence toward the necessary but traumatic changes taking place in that country.

They accepted the need for some whites to be destroyed by the changes taking place, explaining to me that "if their positions and privileges are not taken away, there can be no change," adding "yet, we hurt for those who are chosen; they are our friends and have done nothing uniquely wrong. They, like us, have merely participated in and enjoyed the privileges that went with being white South Africans."

Throughout the weekend we spent together, we toured Charleston, ate in fine restaurants, shopped at the local markets, and talked about the costs of healing. My friend, a black woman, was dubious about the then-ongoing healing hearings in South Africa. She felt that the whites confessing past evils toward blacks were largely specious, and her white guests agreed.

The couple's perspective on the truthfulness and contrition of white South Africans toward apartheid was insightful. They intuitively understood the peculiar problem that nonrelinquished power poses for the psychology of healing. Indeed, their stance resonates fully with the ironic truthfulness in Bishop Tutu's confession with respect to the hearings. Tutu observed that their relative failure was due to the need to obtain contrition and compassion from a minority that still had the power to destroy the proceedings, to undermine the nonviolent and democratic transformation of South Africa.

The bishop's insight requires a special capacity, the ability to accept the vulnerability of the less powerful and to remain hopefully active in the pursuit of equity and justice. Like Mandela before him, Bishop Tutu has attained a kind of racial healing that comes only with psychologically working through this vulnerability. My South African friends, however, are dwelling in the pain of loss and the fear of change. It is difficult to yield to vulnerability under such conditions, and the escape back into power positions (whiteness) becomes especially tempting. In this final chapter, I explore a variety of themes, often as meditations, pertinent to the psychology and pedagogy of healing. I begin with the notion of healing.

On the Nature and Psychology of Healing

What is healing? *To heal* means "to mend, restore, or make whole." The first two definitions of this word imply a prior state of unity or oneness. Healing here means solving the problems that led to the breakdown in relations—values, beliefs, caring—thereby enabling a sense of wholeness. The third definition of the concept of healing—making whole—does not necessarily imply a prior state of unity. It does, however, suggest movement toward unity. In each of these first two definitions of healing is the sense that the breakdown in relations occurred as a result of a violation of some form. Someone was injured.

As implied in these descriptions of healing, the injured and injuring parties are reunited when apology, atonement, and forgiveness have been worked through. While many situations calling for healing are simple and clear-cut, many others are not. Often, there already are socially prescribed procedures for bringing about healing; the involved persons need only commit themselves to asking for and granting forgiveness. Sometimes, however, the society itself lacks an understanding of, or commitment to, doing, "the right things" needed to attain wholeness. This is especially true when unity never truly existed and/or restoration of the past cannot lead to wholeness. Consider the case of minorities in the United States. Inequality, discrimination, and oppression have been enduring forces in the history of this country. What passed for "wholeness" or "unity" was, in fact, a forced oneness: people and groups were locked into a pecking order (much like a caste system) and learned to participate with or relate to others according to prescribed rules and institutionalized systems of control, such as big business, government, and the criminal justice system. Under this arrangement, healing among nonequals was impossible. For healing to occur, one must be able to express one's feelings openly. Of course, this is not a "all or nothing" affair; some people do find ways and means of healing even under less than optimal conditions, and circumstances do change from time to time, thereby allowing degrees of healing. Nonetheless, whether partial or complete, ultimately healing must give birth to mutual respect and care and the shared vulnerability of equals.

This presents us with a pair of paradoxes. The first is the idea that one can violate what one has defined as essential to one's sense or understanding of self: a master violating a slave, a fisherman violating a fish, a cat violating a bird. In each of these examples, one identity is closely bound to the other in some critical way, a way seen as crucial to the existence of the other. What is paradoxical is that at various times and under differing conditions, humans have denied masters, fishermen, and cats access to these defining others. So slavery is abolished; fishermen are fined for taking too many fish; and cats chased away from the family's pet canary.[1]

The second paradox is related to the first: the loss of identity accompanying a societal renegotiation of identity brings about a shared sense of violation, one for which both parties feel a need for justice, vindication, and renewal. I can illustrate this by returning to the prologue. There I described how my South African friends grieved for both the injustices of apartheid for black South Africans and the injustices endured by their fellow white South Africans who were chosen to be the "losers" or "sacrificial lambs" in order that some black South Africans could enter the "mainstream."

These two paradoxes of healing can be heard in the conversations of those caught in the throes of social changes such as racial and gender liberation. Unfortunately, too often they are not discussed and resolved. A closer examination of them can, nonetheless, illuminate the psychology of healing.

The Phenomenology of Healing

The term *phenomenology* has a special meaning in psychology and philosophy; in fact, it has many meanings. I chose to use it here because I want to highlight the importance of one of the meanings central to this term in its various contexts: its focus, in this instance, on the self-understanding and understanding of the community/society of healing-engaged persons. That is, how is healing experienced and/or described by those called on "to heal"? I precede my answer to this question with a brief story. Several years ago, during a group presentation by four white females, I "lost it." The scene was an all too familiar one: The assignment had been to make a presentation dealing with minority women's educational challenges. The four white females presenting this topic provided a good treatment of educational challenges faced by white women, but when asked about the absence of any discussion about black women or other minority women, they claimed they had no knowledge of them. Because this happened almost every semester that I taught this course and their response was one frequently observed and critiqued in the critical race literature (Gresson 1995; Hull, Scott and Smith 1982), I took great pains to ensure that they would not neglect the very groups the topic was designed to cover. So, when this group failed to deal with the topic as instructed, I "lost it."

For me, their refusal was a form of violation: students have an obligation to cover the course material according to the rules of the teacher. Their refusal to do so was more than a mere student neglect or even an individual decision to say no. Their actions, for me, paralleled the arrogance of the oppressor. In class, I dealt with this behavior. I criticized their particular behavior as a failure to follow instructions. I also related it to a habitual neglect of minority women by white females, citing one classic saying of black feminists that "all the blacks are men, all the women are white."

Later, the four women came to my office to apologize for failing to cover the topic. I also apologized for getting so emotional and further explained the reason for my passion. A few days later, two of the four returned to my office: they were upset. Upon reflection, they felt that I had singled them out by raising my objection in class rather than privately in my office. They agreed that they had been told what to cover and that they had failed to do so but still felt I had humiliated them. (For them, I, too, had committed a societal violation. This is an important matter for the issue of democratic education and is significant in the emergent discourse on anti-oppressive education. I return to this theme more fully in a later section of the chapter.) I asked them what they wanted me to do. They said I should apologize in front of the class. Given my values as a democratic, radical educator, I agreed. I would do so during the next class period. Both their request and my consent represented to me a mutually understood sense of shared vulnerability. They had initially cowered under the pressure of the teacher-student authoritarian relationship under which they had grown up and to which they largely subscribed as prospective educators. This was their vulnerability. But I teach from a position of relative equity about what is known and what is knowable. This epistemological radicalism on my part has informed both my scholarship (1977, 1978) and my pedagogy (1990, 1997). Moreover, my personal persuasiveness was largely due to a "post" perspective that acknowledged their "authority" as subjects despite their student status (1995). In addition, I claimed the right to tell them about my "minority perspective" as a fellow human being, and I challenged the dominant "official knowledge" (Spring 1995) from this perspective that acknowledged the integrity of subjective experience even given the fact of so-called cumulative knowledge. Thus I too was vulnerable, and this is generally how I saw the situation.

Still, in preparing to address this matter in class, I found myself smiling at the situation: historically, a black man had few occasions to tell white females they needed to know anything about minority children; whatever whites chose to do or not to do was sanctioned by society. It was an accident of history—the radical social and cultural changes of the 1960s and since—that had placed us in this ironic dance of agency. Still, when I finally came before the class to address the situation, I had concluded that a mere apology would fail to honestly address "what did occur" or what I felt the situation merited in regards to an apology. And so I linked my apology to a discussion of the difference between *humiliation* and *humility*. It seemed to me that in this case, humiliation was the result of these students feeling personally responsible for the broader racial situation. My failure, and it was definitely such, was permitting my own frustration as a victim of racism to overflow and negatively influence my position as the teacher. Ideally, I should have downplayed their failure to do what was asked of them during the class period and saved it for a private audience with them. In so doing, I perhaps would have fulfilled my own personal and pedagogical obligation. But reflecting on my failure and confronting my own reluctance to speak before the entire class, I was struck by these students' refusal to assume any public blame. Initially, they had said that I had not overstepped my bounds during the critique and that they understood my frustration. But later, for two of them at least, my actions had assumed the weight of an oppressive violation.[2] The conversation in my office did not resolve the problem; they were not healed. They did not feel right. They needed a particular transaction to take place in the classroom.

This story reveals the "phenomenological" character of healing. Healing is a feeling, an emotion. As such, it has both a physiological and a cognitive dimension. The physiological is the bodily aspect, the tightening of the jaws, the pounding of the head, the lump in the throat, the pain in the stomach, the compulsion to move toward or away from the other. For this bodily response to occur, however, one has to have a mediating lens, a way of understanding what things do and do not constitute a violation for one. This is the cognitive dimension. In this episode, both the white women and I were physiologically involved; we each had something at stake in the multiculturalism discourse. We each shared a sense of violation at the global and the classroom levels; we each harbored a vision of the other as a "carrier of bad blood." The request for an apology exposed a hidden wound related to this bad blood between us. This "bad blood" is the cultural psychology of racism (Kovel 1970) and sexism (Bederman 1995) in the United States.

The request for an apology implies more. Some might say it is simply an insistence to be treated as "an individual" free of the stigma of "spoiled identity" (Goffman 1963). Even though no one, except perhaps the powerful, can realistically imagine a place beyond the gaze of the other, there is another, thornier objection here: the request for an apology represents an attempt to renegotiate an identity's value even as one is advancing the privileges of that identity. Both I and the students had something at stake: a belief/feeling that we were in the right. None of us involved could quite accept the full responsibility for the exchange even after admitting a level of "wrong doing" or responsibility.

This episode suggests that healing pertains to both personal identity and subjective understanding of social justice. It is not a simple matter of the facts of the situation. Because this is so, healing occurs through a working back and forth between contrasting, sometimes contradictory, ideas of the facts and what is important. Healing is therefore a *dialectical* matter. I will now elaborate on this quality of healing.

Healing as a Dialectic: White Diversity Leadership as an Illustration

Healing is dialectical because it takes place in the presence of two power-ful contradictions or uneasy tensions. First, there is the need to accept the experience of violation and a loss of something cherished. Second, what-ever is recoverable can be only a partial recovery. The well-known expres-sions "suck it up" and "get over it" point to this aspect of healing as a com-promised outcome at its best. Thus healing means confronting the original sacrifice (and loss) that led to the fractured wholeness that is now being "made whole" through yet another fracturing. This is why the lan-guage of, say, white racial recovery generated notions like "reverse ra-cism," "white male as victim of affirmative action," and "black racism." These speech events and experiences signal that healing is perhaps psychologically problematic from the start, especially when the original violation occurred in the service of identity formation. That is, to ask me to deny my "whiteness" as a condition of "equality" when my identity as "white" is predicated on my "superiority" is problematic. The request that one stops being a "man" of a certain kind so that another can be a "woman" in more liberating ways can be a difficult request to deliver: what kind of man can/ought one to become and can this be achieved by fiat? The two students who wanted me to apologize to them are but echoes of a more recent group, white males, making a parallel claim re-garding "humiliation." Reporting on a diversity seminar by whites for whites, William Atkinson writes:

> If the goal of engaging white men in diversity is to succeed, the attitudes of white males will not be the only things that will need to change. . . . [One participant said] "One of the most troublesome concerns I have is that, as we continue to do 'white men's work,' there is still much work for women and people of color to do on themselves and their beliefs about white men." (2001: 5)

Implicit in this insistence is the idea that white men are not what white men appear to be to the other. This re-positioning of self in relation to other is what I felt with the female students who at once *acted* outside the established rules of the game yet insisted that I recognize the rules of the game. The near absolute disconnect white people now exhibit with re-spect to historical racism is suggestive in this incipient conversation of fe-male and minority "imperfection" and "violation" of white males. Inter-estingly, while I suggest a convergence between my white female students and white males espousing this gender/racial victimhood, white women are especially criticized as the new oppressors of men. I have already cited several examples of this trend in earlier chapters. Nonetheless, the belief that women and minorities must act upon themselves reveals important clues to the dialectical nature of healing discourse and dynamics. This can be seen in recent efforts to include white men in the diversity leadership training business. I want to examine further the report on this diversity leadership seminar as a way of clarifying the parameters of the dialectic.

White Diversity and Diversity Leadership

Recognition of white racism as a nonessential part of white identity, whether fact or fantasy, allows for the very self-display that Michael Apple (1998) warns against. But it is on us nonetheless. We see this everywhere, especially in affirmative action and diversity efforts. In a manner reminiscent of the "white power" slogans of the 1970s and 1980s, there has been increasing insistence on including whites in the equation of equity efforts. This is significant because whites do not generally perceive their racial benefits; rather, it is good societal management. It is likely that all societies that work well manage to move unself-consciously from idea to actuality. Such is the case with whites in Western societies that have built up notions of individual and collective identity by devaluing "the other." It is in this context that the move toward white preeminence in diversity training can be best appreciated. Whites can now teach diversity, and they can participate—as peers if not as masters—in clarifying and conquering the barriers to greater democratic unity and inclusion in society and institutions.

This need to distance the white self from negativity is understandable, but it is also a condition for many whites to join the twenty-first-century diversity discourse. Consequently, white diversity is evolving from the insistence that racism is essentially dead in America. Buttressed by civil rights laws that sometimes work and a notably black presence within the American middle class, white diversity is an insistence on partnership with the "weaker" negotiating side of diversity initiatives.

William Atkinson is instructive here in his article about white men as full diversity partners. In particular, he reports on a consortium of three diversity consulting firms: EqualVoice in Minneapolis; Industry Consulting Group in Portland, Oregon; and Integral Coaching and Consultation in Herndon, Virginia. The topics for these groups include the domination of the diversity coordinator position in most organizations by minority males or females. "It is rarely a white male." Why should it be?

Michael Welp, a principal at EqualVoice, believes that for the diversity movement to reach the next level of effectiveness and change in organizations, white men must know a lot about diversity. "Most of what they know about diversity comes from women and people of color, which places a lot of pressure on these groups," he says. "White men need to learn how to engage each other, so that women and people of color don't have to do the whole job of educating us." (Atkinson, 2001: 1)

What does this mean? That white men don't now know how to engage with one another? What is at stake in minorities assuming the leadership of diversity leadership? What is the pressure on minorities for assuming this leadership role? The idea of full inclusion for white males in the new drama is important. Feeling left out from the access to work is symbolic:

> As a white male doing diversity work for 12 years, I noted early on that diversity managers were women or people of color 99 percent of the time. In fact, I found that I often was unable to get work in corporations because I was a white male. I'd always hear the question, "What do you know about diversity?" (Atkinson 2001: 1)

Ironically, this consortium sees as one of its main tasks teaching white males that they are not merely individuals but part of a culture and a group. Haskell, my close friend of nearly thirty years, certainly sees himself as an individual rather than as a group member. But in large measure, what allows this to happen is white power. The capacity to redesign the structure of diversity initiatives may simultaneously accomplish the tasks of the "enlightenment" and "recontainment" of minority momentum.

Recognizing the typical inability or refusal of white males to own racial privilege, these workshop organizers have several goals, including helping white men recognize their role in "the work" of diversity. "We want to eliminate the existing inequity of people thinking that women and people of color are the only ones who know about diversity, and therefore expecting them to teach everyone else," says Bill Proudman, president of Inclusivity Consulting Group. He continues, "We want to help white males see themselves and other white males as partners in 'the work'" (Atkinson, 2001:3). Another goal is to create inclusive organizations. Thus Jo Ann Morris, a principal consultant with Integral Coaching and Consultation in Herndon, Virginia, reflects:

> The workshop's ultimate goal is to facilitate a strategic view of what it means to be an inclusive organization . . . We look at what it means to have white men feel grounded enough and safe enough about what diversity is

for them, individually and collectively, so that diversity is not just about everyone else except them. . . . (Atkinson, 2001: 3)

For decades, women and minorities were recognized as the victims of injustice and inequality and the logical leaders to train whites in general and white men in particular about the nature and process of diversity enhancement through affirmative action and other inclusive practices. This development enhanced both minority wealth and importance in the business world, thus yielding a dialectic: white men should also profit from the wisdom of inclusion, even though they dominate the social order in a manner that begets the initial inclusion mandate. (It is perhaps already clear that the discussion of anti-oppressive teaching as potentially oppressive overlaps with this logic.)

Healing thus requires a dual, almost simultaneous admission of loss. Society fails to deal adequately with the nature of the loss and the required "terms of re-endearment." It abandons individuals and collectivities to make subjective sense of its politics and policies but offers no consolation, no sense of justice. It is wholly pragmatic and unethical, yet it is infinitely moral, for its agenda is saving the collective-as-is. This is especially true in matters of social justice that have built up over centuries of mistrust, misdeeds, and mixed ideologies of who is blameworthy and who is righteous. Given this understanding of healing, we also may have a better grasp of the more psychological dynamics of healing as these have evolved around race and related matters.

Notes on the Psychology of Healing

And we are fundamentally inclined to claim that the falsest judgments . . . are the most indispensable for us . . . that renouncing false judgments would mean renouncing life and a denial of life. To recognize untruth as a condition of life—that certainly means resisting accustomed value feelings in a dangerous way; and a philosophy that risks this would by that token alone place itself beyond good and evil. (Friedrich Nietzsche, 1966: 12)

A philosopher by temperament and vocation, Nietzsche has been recognized by many as a premier psychologist. When I read these lines from his 1886 treatise *Beyond Good and Evil*, I became fixated on a particular vision or sensation: we are trapped, even though we must struggle to escape. Less mysteriously, these lines meant for me that the pursuit of truth, however defined, is a task only partly undertaken in our best interest. It may satisfy certain of our needs, but it will likely severely test others. Healing, guided or cautioned by this ambivalence toward knowing, pursues at least two psychological goals: mourning and mending.

Mourning: "Exorcising" the Loss

In *Passage to Ararat*, Michael Arlen "describes weeping and denial of the past as two ways of mourning the genocidal war of the Turks which destroyed the Armenians. This mourning cannot come to an end; the loss is too great to be learned from, or to be forgotten" (Lyman 1981: 58). We have to hurt, to cry. Mourning implies a time or period of dwelling in pain. The educative outcome of this visit with the pain of loss is greater insight into and appreciation of what is actuality and necessity. Presumably, from here one is able to move forward: wounded, yes, but better for it.

The fear and uncertainty of what to do next may lead one to surrender to and enter a shared pursuit with the other.[3] This new, shared journey brings with it the possibility of genuine healing. But there may also be a positive—from some perspectives—adjustment in which appropriation of the desired loss or absence is pursued (see Bettleheim 1962).

In the introduction to this chapter, I noted that white South Africans generally acknowledge that the black numerical majority and the resulting black South African leadership have put the whites living there on a very different growth trajectory than they are in the United States. This difference, moreover, amounts to a different felt need for and pursuit of healing than that recognized as a need in contemporary America. Thus, unable to find partial healing through a national recognition of racial wrongdoing, many African Americans display mourning behavior similar to that found by Arlen and the Armenians. Just last night, for example, I was sitting in a black middle-class bar frequented by middle-aged African American men. One, a retired Baltimore policeman, was "bleeding," even though he had retired from the force well and alive. He expressed a hatred for the United States and called several of us "Uncle Toms" because we professed love for the country and accepted the idea that not all white people are evil. After the noise died down and he and I were able to talk more quietly, I saw the pain, the hurt beneath the bravado and hatred. He now lamented his participation on an inner-city police force that had exposed him to much abuse from both whites and blacks. He despaired over his own frustrated ambitions for promotion and success that had been damaged by his attempt to be "his own man" and a "human being" toward his fellow African Americans. He grieved openly about the ravages of racism in his professional life. And, when I was able to listen to his pain, affirm the injustice of his suffering, and the "screwed up human condition," he seemed a changed man. He exhaled. Then he thanked me and quietly left the bar.

Somewhere from my subconscious, a thought appeared: somewhere I had recently read something linked to my bar experience. Later, I found the passage in Lyman's essay:

> But how is this reconciliation of the private and the historical achieved in one's own life? The tension between theory and practice becomes a chasm of alienation when private sorrows are suffered silently, unredeemed by collective reflection and response. Yet many contemporary voices speak out of this alienation. These voices are texts, fragments of memories from the unresolved past that cannot be mourned and eventually give way to peaceful recollection or determined action; that past haunts the present and the future will capitulate the past. (1981: 56)

The problem is psychological. The need is psychological (though the vehicle is ultimately political). This means that the "logic" or procedure for the desired change pertains to the mental and emotional worlds. Mourning is the expression of this logic. When it is successful, things fall into place. When it is unsuccessful, things are forced into *some* place. This is the very tricky business of healing. If the terms for healing are "unfair"—peace on my terms—then there may be a semblance of healing, but in Lyman's words, the "past haunts the present and the future will capitulate the past" (1981: 56).

We must understand that white pain, a form of mourning, has given way to a series of "determined actions" that I call recovery strategies. These actions have achieved a certain consolation for many whites, but at the expense of those who sense that some injustice has been perpetrated on them. The 2000 election symbolized this, and it will likely be decades before we can fully grasp this fact or realize that something on the order of the attack on September 11 had to occur to bring some form of healing to America. Thus, for some people, mending, the other great pillar of healing, may yield "breakage" for others.

Mending: "Plotting" a Recovery

Emerging from the break, mending pertains to those ideas, actions, and emotions that transform the separation, replacing disunity with unity, twoness with oneness. The dictionary is instructive here with its various definitions of *mending*: "repair," "amend," "correct errors," "improve," "reform," "heal." But the dictionary does not convey an idea of *the sacred*, although for humans this concept/vision is crucial to the attainment of "repair-ness."

Because it may be inequitable, mending is a dialectical unfolding. Viewed in this way, healing is perpetual; the end state is illusion. Only death can yield a final mending. Pain and violence often accompany what seems to be a "nearly mended" situation because the terms of repair are not free of the violating formative ideas that caused the initial infraction. I mention again the controversy surrounding the proposed Firemen's Memorial in New York City. The need of some white men to challenge the proposed forefronting of a diverse firefighter icon reveals that healing draws on problematic values.

A picture of three white males hoisting the American flag is a healing image. A statue of white, black, and "colored" firemen hoisting the flag also is a healing image. Some would argue that a truly unified nation would have no difficulty in choosing one rather than the other. But this is the challenge: whose notions of mending images will make for a soothed soul? Norman O. Brown wrote:

> The external enemy is (part of) ourselves, projected; our own badness, banished. The only defense against an internal danger is to make it an external danger: then we can fight it; and are ready to fight it, since we have succeeded in deceiving ourselves into thinking it is no longer us. (1966: 162)

According to Brown, we are motivated to act aggressively, surgically, only when we have distanced the "bad," the "cancer," "the axis of evil," from ourselves. This is a core deception of ourselves by ourselves. There is something familiar or "truthful" in the white male's query to the black male marching on Washington for a day of atonement: "Are you atoning for your crimes against me?" Whatever the flaws in this query and the thinking behind it, I sense a wisdom of sorts; it is the sense that all are called to examine and change the conversation about inclusion. It is also the uttering of a profound fact: seizing one's own human potential may undermine another's in ways that lead to the belief that atonement is required even though one has only acted to take back an original "birthright."

The psychology and pedagogy of healing bring us face to face with ourselves. We are implicated in life; we take and we give. We eat to live, and in this act we sacrifice others. Under capitalism, in the type of democracy we have attained to date, the symbolic and substantive consumption of others is inevitable. We are, moreover, only partly motivated—and, even then, under duress—to be otherwise. Enron, Andersen, WorldCom, and Martha Stewart stand as only the tip of the iceberg of our guilt, greed, and destructive proclivity. We blanch at the losses perpetrated by Arthur Andersen and the Enron empire, yet we daily watch to see whether our own stocks—personal value—will suffer. And we pray for a quick, complete recovery of the Dow Jones.

Susan Langer wrote in her final, monumental work, *Mind: An Essay on Human Feeling:*

> The original motivation of sacrifice was, I believe, a sense of danger in the performance of an autonomous overt act that changed the agent's situation. Any such act, initiated by a single or multiple agent, is an exercise of mental power, and as such demonstrates the individuating activity of mind. . . . Something had been autonomously done; to restore the biological balance something would have to be yielded; and the readiest symbol of submission to the claim of the greater, ancestral life force is to give up some precious thing to it, i.e., to make sacrifice. . . . Sacrifice is *par excellence* the means of restoring the ethnic balance; and in this capacity it is never without a basic sense of loss and surrender. (1984: 133)

Langer's description is reminiscent of Dostoyevsky, Freud, Reich, and others who have struggled with the question of crime, guilt, and punishment with respect to the human condition. Recall the opening epigraph: Bishop Desmond Tutu's concession to the power of the white South Africans is ironic, for to achieve healing, even to approach some semblance of reconciliation, he and the black majority must sacrifice to achieve "an ethnic balance." This requires of him and us both loss and surrender even in our victory. This is the paradoxical psychopedagogical wisdom of those who understand humanity's plight in terms of identity and power.

Reflections on Healing

In the remainder of this chapter, I offer several thoughts that invite reflection on the topic of healing. If healing is about both mourning and mending, then it requires conscious reflection on our thoughts and our actions.

Toward Healing: Anger, Silence, and Vulnerability

In 1981, I came across an article that made a great impact on my thinking about white anger. Peter Lyman, writing in *The Socialist Review*, examined the interface of silence, *ressentiment*, and the politics of anger. What struck me so deeply about this essay, in many ways ahead of its time, was the blending of so many critical notions from feminist, Marxist, and radical perspectives with regard to the plight of middle-class whites. He (1981: 55) begins his essay with a passage from Adrienne Rich's *On Lies, Secrets, and Silence:*

> As I thrust my hand deeper into the swirl of this stream—history, nightmare, accountability—I feel the current angrier and more multiform than the surface shows. There is fury here, and terror, but there is also power, power not to be had without the terror and the fury. We need to go beyond rhetoric or evasion into that place in ourselves, to feel the force of all we have been trying—without success—to skim across. (1981: 55)

In an end note, Lyman explains the source and significance of this passage:

> This passage ends the essay . . . , which discusses the silence that isolates lesbians and black women, and the racism that divides them. It is a kind of therapeutic writing that recovers political power from the fragmentation and depression that is the result of suppressed and repressed anger, but in addition, it is a political writing that attempts to overcome the defects of anger and find a way from the self-righteousness of anger to a more general understanding of the structures that create it. (1981: 72)

For me, the passage from Rich was powerful, but that from Lyman was even more so because he was moving beyond the issues that Rich identified specifically for the marginalized lesbian and black female to the white middle class. Focusing on Vietnam, Lyman reviews the poetry created by many of these veterans (remember, the year was 1980 and we had not reached a period where we could gloss over the painful sorrows and emotions).

> Guilty memories traumatize the present with anxiety as a form of self-punishment. And although guilt is part of the source of this poetry, it is more than a poetry of guilt; it is a political poetry. . . . The question of the meaning of the war in Vietnam for America has not been answered, and has been shifted from the polity to the soldier through a conspiracy of silence which transforms a political question into psychological symptom, a problem of veterans' benefits and "drug-related violence." (1981: 57)

Written more than two decades ago, Lyman's words remind us that glossing over the complex cultural and political challenges in our society leaves us vulnerable to being decentered, being untruthful. Consequently, so the Freudians tell us, the repressed conflicts seep out, uncalled and uncontrolled. To uncover what we have concealed, then, is essential to repairing the real damages rather than the fabricated ones that require considerable, though perhaps less courageous, remediation.

The Internet and Racial (Non) Healing

On Thursday, April 11, 2002, an e-mail sent to me as a chain letter began with "Racism at Harvard Law."

Dear Family and Friends,

In recent weeks, members of the Black Law Students Association of Harvard Law School have been the targets of overt racial hostility. The tension began when a first year student published his class notes to the Internet: his notes refer to Black people using the term "nigs." When we requested that his notes be removed from the school's website, other students e-mailed in protest, defending their "right" to refer to Black people as "nigs," "niggers," and insisting that Black people, as a race, prove ourselves so that we won't be called "niggers." As individuals and as a group we have attempted to seek redress for our grievances from the administration. This process has ultimately proved unsatisfactory as offending professors have gone uncensored and the student perpetrators have gone unpunished. The situation has escalated because of the administration's lack of response. Students have dispersed flyers with anti-semitic and anti-Black statements; professors have openly defended students that express their desire to use the n-word whenever referring to Black people. One professor has even gone so far as to express to his class that Blacks have contributed nothing to Tort law. One student organization disrespectfully dismissed a young Black woman from its office believing her to be a member of the community seeking legal services. All the while, we have been trying to work through diplomatic, administrative means to resolve these situations but have been met with resistance from the administration and token apologies. We have resolved that we cannot accept this disrespect any longer. In light of the university's disrespect of us as a people we believe that a time for action has arrived. In the days to come, the Black Law Students of Harvard Law School will be taking affirmative action to seek redress for our grievances. We are composing a letter of our grievances and demands, contacting the national media, and planning public demonstrations in protest of the treatment we have experienced. We are being joined by La Alianza (Hispanic students of the law school) and the African Law Students Association. I ask that you would pray for me and for all of the students that are coming together in a statement of solidarity. I must confess to you that these events have taken a personal toll on me as well as my classmates. We are in need of your prayers and your support. If you are an alum of Harvard University, please contact me if you are able to lend a helping hand. We need the support of alumni in a big way. Most of all, please keep us in your prayers as the need for institutional change is tremendous and the time before exams is short. To be sure, the odds are stacked against us. Without a doubt, I know that God is with us in this time of trial. (1 Peter 1: 6). Until later, please take care and God bless.

Some years back, the Black Muslim leader Louis Farrakhan named the Internet as a source of liberation against injustice and tyranny. Whether or not this will prove to be the case, the Internet has clearly emerged as an important site for racial healing and hurting. The preceding e-mail is an example. It invites some to join in a multiracial coalition against the persistence of racism; it may also incite those who might be named "racists" to further coalesce against a perceived threat.

Still, those sites that promote healing can be extremely instructive and inspirational. Consider the 1990s organization Healing Racism, Inc. Naming its mission the elimination of racism in the United States through grassroots community development, this site overviews a range of healing strategies. Its programs include "ally building" as a way to help healing. Franklin Sonn, South African ambassador to the United Nations, is quoted on the site as saying:

And it's also impossible to go to healing without knowing the past, because the past is a funny thing. It comes up at the most awkward moments, when you least expect it, and then it disrupts the process of healing and reconciliation. But a very important point also to mention is that our government never expected this to be an easy process, never expected that the outcome would be pleasant. It was a painful process to start off with, and it, therefore, took enormous courage for us as nation to face our past in the manner that it did. But, . . . it's out now, and now we can start with the healing process.

Once again we are reminded that healing must confront head-on the perceived injustices. Even if these recollections are ultimately abandoned as "real," "reasonable," or "relevant" matters, their past reality and relevance must be accepted.

A powerful story illustrating this point was told by Bob Lupton in "The Great Racial Divide . . . An Opportunity for Healing," from *The Gospel and Our Culture* newsletter (December 1995 www.netdoor.com/rronline):

Our black staff erupted in spontaneous applause and joyful cheers, our white staff sat in stunned silence. . . . The following morning when I arrived at the office my first phone call was from Albert Love, a black minister friend. After brief social exchanges, he went directly to the matter that prompted his call. It was the O.J. verdict. Knowing that most African-Americans could understand the justice in the jury's decision while many whites would see it as a miscarriage of justice, Albert wanted to prevent this difference of perspective from further fragmenting the community of faith. He sensitively affirmed any feelings that I might be experiencing that were different from his own. . . . How reconciling his sensitivity! I was aware that by this thoughtful act my need to generalize blame had been diminished.

Recall Mandela's historic healing gesture after his maltreatment. Albert, like Mandela, reached out beyond his own pain and woundedness to his wounded white friend. One may sense that the wounded majority-group person may feel a pain so great that the minority person must be the one to initiate sensitivity. Notice here the equality we are implying: whites feel like victims, like minorities, and thus require care because they really do have relatively more power. This is a powerful irony. It rehearses earlier reflections on the dialectics of healing, the possibility that "fairness" as a logic has secondary importance to reestablishing a shared moment of "well-being."

There are continual efforts to make healing work even when we do not readily encounter them. The range of initiatives, moreover, suggests that the initiative is serious. Thus we learn from the Internet of educational healing efforts such as the Oaks Academy, which opened in Indianapolis in 1998 (*StarNews.com* September 8, 1998), and is described as "a new school designed to bring racial reconciliation to the inner city."

In Pasadena, California, a church held a racial reconciliation weekend (June 22 and 23, 1996), facilitated by the Center for Healing of Racism in Houston. The Center's co-executive director, Barbara Hacker, explains:

> Racial reconciliation is not about making people feel guilty. It's not about making them feel responsible for something someone else did. It's not about stirring up the trouble of the past. It's about focusing on the future. It is about coming out of denial and acknowledging what happened. In our country horrible things happened. Slavery happened. Segregation happened. Racial discrimination happened, and it still happens.

The critical importance of these various initiatives and their dominating themes is their resonance with others mentioned elsewhere on Internet sites dealing with healing:

> When we deny things or tell people who are experiencing pain and hurt that they are being too sensitive or that they shouldn't feel that way, or "I didn't do it," "I'm not racist," "I'm not prejudiced"—what we are doing is denying them their feelings, denying them their reality of what they have been experiencing.

Of course, this applies as well to the racist or the target of racism. There is a challenge—a dance of agency, as I have called it—in which individual subjectivities must be recognized, not coddled, condoned, but recognized. Again, Ms. Hacker:

> You don't have to approve or disapprove. You don't have to fix it. You just have to give people space to get it out. And once they've voiced it a healing takes place. . . . The job of the listener is to acknowledge that another has experienced pain. "I'm sorry you have experienced pain."

At Lamb and Lion Ministries (www.lamblion.com), Dennis Pollack writes the following in "Racism and the Church: Still a Need for Healing":

> Racism is a blight upon our nation. Not only the attitude of whites toward blacks, but blacks toward whites, Orientals toward Hispanics, and society in general toward Jews. Many conservative Christians are quick to denounce abortion and homosexuality, but are strangely silent on the issue of racism. It is almost as though racism has become a "conservatively correct" issue to overlook. (1996: 3)

The Internet is full of hurt and healing. Marshall McLuhan declared in the mid-twentieth century that "the medium is the message and the massage" and ushered in a new generation of thinking and writing on the power and promise of communications media and technology. The Internet, too, is full of power and promise, an occasion for healing.

September 11 and the "New Humanity" Discourse

Another event arising from the trauma of September 11 was the National Conference for Community and Justice—Race, Ethnicity & Culture, shown on C-Span and hosted by Juan Williams, a journalist and commentator on National Public Radio and Fox News. A theme of this conference was "the new humanity." Many recognized in the violence and devastation of September 11 something beyond the moment. Motivated by different interests and concerns, the pursuit of a new humanity came from diverse thinkers and leaders. For example, among the speakers was the Nation of Islam leader Imam Deem Muhammad:

> We need to think deep into this thing . . . 9/11. Islam did not create that mind . . . the world created that mind. . . . America has a nature to go to the extremes. . . . [we need] a movement for community . . . we are in one room . . . this earth is one earth . . . one community . . . a home for human beings.

Others also spoke of a "new human nature" for man. Reverend Daniel Coughlin, the chaplain of the U.S. House of Representatives, called for a "new look at human nature." Sharifa Alkhateeb, president of the Muslim Education Council, asked, "Whose idea of humanity shall reign? What is the middle point? What can go forth . . . benefit humanity . . . we may reach goals . . . but they won't be good ones." And Bishop Thomas Hoyt, president of the National Council of Churches, declared that we must seek "a willingness to die for humanity."

In these themes on the discourse of humanity, we sense that the pain associated with September 11 propelled many people to examine nonmilitary solutions. To be sure, the displays of might in Afghanistan and Iraq have soothed us to a degree. The specter of the World Trade Center and Pentagon in flames, while put deep into our preconscious, may find some solace in such actions. But there remains a sense that we must find alternative answers. The great challenge is looking into the other's pain and seeing our reflected narrative. This is a task we as yet largely reject. Whether expressed in terms of domestic racial relations and/or international relations, the challenge is much the same: vulnerable confrontation of the shared pain of human evil and destructiveness.

Apology and Reparations to Blacks, White Anger

> [Young white Americans] feel that there is nothing to forgive . . . they are afraid
> of what will come out.
> BISHOP TUTU

A recent Web interview between Marianne Williamson, author of *The Healing of America*, and Mary Nurrie Stearns, editor of *Personal Transformation*, reveals this difficulty. When asked how the "cultural atonement" linked to America's slavery past could be achieved, Williamson observed:

> There are many ways such a ritual could be performed. If we wanted to do it, we could come up with a way. When Representative Tony Hall of Ohio submitted a bill in the House of Representatives suggesting that Congress apologize for slavery, there was such an outcry the bill didn't have a chance of going forward. Newt Gingrich called a congressional apology for slavery mere "emotional symbolism." He asked if it would teach one child to read. I say to you, it would, because it would remove some heavy blocks to our awareness of love.

For a healing discourse to have a chance of working in the American dreamscape, it ultimately comes back to power and how one negotiates with specific individuals who comply with power's hegemonic hold, that is, the hold based on our personal and subjective surrender to the material goods and substantive freedoms we enjoy as "winners" in the American dreamscape.

Beyond this, one has to be able to overcome a certain disassociation. This greater barrier has a characteristic form: "I have done nothing to anybody—the past is not upon my head." This pervasive and passionate sentiment is uttered from the depths of the soul. From the mouths of those identified as heirs of the powerful and dominant, these words issue from persons determined to be fair, forthright, and productive citizens. Still, I am troubled by them. My concern is that these utterances will delay the transformative shifts we need if society is truly to become more democratic and righteous.

President Nelson Mandela observed: "If the pain has often been unbearable and the revelations shocking to all of us, it is because they, indeed, bring us the beginnings of a common understanding of what happened and a steady restoration of the nation's humanity" (www.pbs.org, Online News Hour: Truth Commission, October 29, 1998). But contemporary Americans refuse to confront this past, rejecting healing and nurturing the restoration of racist sentiments. Consider the anti-apology efforts of David Horowitz as discussed at the CNN.com law center's open forum site by Anthony J. Sebok, professor of law at Brooklyn College and Findlaw columnist:

> Some compared Horowitz's effort to purchase advertising space in college newspapers for what was, in effect, a right-wing editorial with an earlier attempt by a Holocaust denier to purchase advertising space in college newspapers to publicize his extremely bizarre view that the Holocaust was a hoax. . . . Horowitz attempt[s] to set up a sort of balance sheet, to purportedly ascertain which groups benefited from slavery, and how. Horowitz contends that Africans (and other non-Europeans) participated in and benefited from living in the United States, rather than in Africa.

Horowitz reminds us that healing is problematic because emotion and intellect can be separated only when one does not feel an immediate personal threat. Years ago, when reflecting on the question of interminority group coalitions, I argued that we need images of the other and cooperative action that do not reduce our sensitivity to justice for all by falling victim to invidious distinctions and insensibilities (1977, 1978). But Horo-witz has been revealed, exposed, by his willingness to undermine healing through his own reidentification with the "pigs" and "reactionary right" that he once fought against, thus enabling him to achieve a radical hero's status.

If there is no willingness to surrender to the pain of past transgressions, then healing will be perverted, for the aggrieved will be silenced, but live to speak and perhaps rise up again.

Israel, the War on Terror, and the Lesson of Shylock

In my youth, I recall reading somewhere that Shakespeare's tragic drama *The Merchant of Venice* was supposedly evidence that he was anti-Semitic. Personally, I read both Shakespeare and his Jewish character, Shylock, as powerful pedagogues for the pariahs of the world. Shakespeare, whether a real person or a composite of several, was indeed wise regarding the pariah, Shylock, if we see him as a composite of all humans, particularly racial and sexual minorities, who seek "justice" in the "domain of the unjust."

I recently shared my reading of *The Merchant of Venice* with an Israeli acquaintance. He immediately recognized and affirmed my reasoning. Citing the almost fatalistic role of Jews in human history, he declared that Jews had to be tough in order to balance (and here I recall Tevye, from *Fiddler on the Roof*)[4] the contradictions of daily life. Agreeing with my reading of the pariah's paradox, he understood well the dangers and damage, psychic and physical, to one who accepts too deeply the healing terms of the powerful other.

In 2003, American minorities—African Americans, Asian Americans, Hispanic Americans, and so forth—share these dangers with the Israelis. The real advances invite and encourage us not only to forget the past but also to collude in the distortion of the present oppressive character of public life. The Israeli predicament with respect to healing is instructive here. Begin with the given: it is imperative that Israelis have both land and power in order to survive a mean world. How do they get them? They get them through the largesse of the Gentile world that has named Jews the pariah and exploited them politically for thousands of years. Like African Americans and others, Jews are invited to find acceptance by disidentifying with the other and preparing to survive through aggression with the other.

It is not that Arabs are nice, weak, or innocent. It's just that the Israelis have surrendered to hundreds of years of persecution and have accepted yet again—and certainly not unlike many others—the role of "middle minority." This term, common to the sociology of race relations and minorities, refers to those groups whose persecution by more powerful others is mediated and muted by hurting and oppressing others. The ironic significance of this role and its current currency is the recent observation that, since September 11, black oppression has diminished in the wake of increased Arab oppression in the United States.

My point is that the current wave of Israeli (out)rage with Palestinian violence, however understood, resonates with U.S. foreign policy since September 11. The window of opportunity for Israeli activity created by America's "war on terrorism" and invasion of Iraq is transparent. But Israelis, like Shylock, are tragic heroes in the "Christian drama" in which anti-Semitism is forever lurking beneath the surface. Indeed, since I began this discussion some four weeks ago, a crescendo of anti-Israel sentiment has surfaced. I sensed it first on the Internet. Several white supremacy sites simultaneously goad Israelis toward aggression and declare Jews the ultimate "eternal evil."

Then I sensed it among the white media, outraged at the Shylockian arrogance of the Israeli soldiers who dared treat them as soldiers often treat civilians: harshly, unfairly, deadly. Shortly thereafter, even traditional allies were showing discord. For instance, consider UN Secretary General Kofi Annan. According to the *New York Times* (Wednesday, March 13, 2002, A9), he spoke out against Israel despite his strong support of her over the years:

> In the harshest language he has used since the present crisis began 17 months ago, Mr. Annan chastised the Israelis for the use of heavy weapons in civilian areas and called their occupation of Palestinian lands "illegal," demanding Israel's withdrawal.

The extreme vulnerability I speak of is perhaps most fully sensed when we read in the same article that:

> Some Israeli politicians harshly criticized the army for writing identification numbers on the forearms and foreheads of Palestinian prisoners. "It is totally unbearable for me," said Tommy Lapid, a member of Parliament and a survivor of the Nazi camps. "This is something that was done at Auschwitz." (A8)

This attack against Israel exposes the vulnerability of the underdog. It also tells us how the underdog, especially when colluding with power, can be recast in the role of villain by those in power. Hence, in a response to the Israeli claim that its actions paralleled the U.S. attack on Afghanistan, Richard A. Boucher, a spokesman for the State Department, said the administration respected Israel's "right of defense" but added, "We continue to be very troubled by Israeli Defense Force actions." He called it "imperative" that the army "exercise the utmost restraint and discipline to avoid further harm to civilians or worsening the humanitarian situation" (A8). Nor is the emergent anti-Israeli sentiment restricted to a single newspaper or writer. The *Baltimore Sun* noted that Israeli checkpoints were undermining Middle Eastern peace: "There have been well-documented incidents of harassment and lack of discipline. Pregnant women have been denied access to maternity wards, the sick from medical care, and mourners from funerals. Young men are arbitrarily taken and beaten and young women sexually harassed" (March 10, 2002, 5F). The point is that Israel is behaving unwisely but possibly in the only way it can, given its "tracking." Thus, by April 2002, the media had begun reporting a rising tide of anti-Semitism in Europe. In a vaguely disguised rhetoric, President Bush chastised Israel. In Europe, faint hints of a resurging anti-Semitism were taking center stage. These actions suggest that healing can be compromised when the rationale for violence used to achieve the upper hand can be easily turned back against one.

Understanding the Cultural Psychology of Nonhealing

Healing, particularly that aimed at racial and other societal injustices, requires one to turn away from a cultural defense mechanism, one that has been socialized into the citizenry, one in which both victim and victimizer share in the construction of domination and the resulting need for healing—the return of "shared firstness" (Gresson 1982).

What is needed is a massive, global change in the nature of the society. It is evident in the fact that the United States, having declared a "war on terrorism," has exposed the complexity of the ideas preceding and following the war campaign, for instance, in trying to establish a "coalition of aggrieved nations" and then insisting that the United States will act unilaterally when and if it needs to. This dualism says something not only about our society but also about our historical representation of aggressive action (Slotkin 1973) and the ways that individuals are socialized into complicity with this system.

Notions like "axis of evil" fail even in the domestic situation in which parallel terrorisms exist. For example, we have largely forgotten Timothy McVeigh and the mentality that led seemingly decent young white men to kill in a manner similar to that of the September 11 attacks and to receive the support of domestic militia in a manner similar to that of some Arab communities after September 11.

In all cases, these acts are horrifying, and they all were committed by human beings convinced that their actions were righteous. Such "axes of evil" are not isolated phenomena. The anti-abortion contingency, for instance, is notable here. Identified by former President Bill Clinton as perpetrators of "domestic terrorism," these groups, like the Army of God (see save the babies.com), are all around us, and their thinking is instructive with respect to the psychopedagogy of healing. As Bob Lokey, an anti-abortion activist, stated in a documentary on the movement, "There is a point at which your emotions can only take so much." The activists' thinking is cogent: "Stop abortion with a bullet, a bomb . . . you stop abortion on demand."

I have just finished watching a 1999 terrorist movie starring Jeff Bridges and Tim Robbins. The terrorists win. They are white men and women and children seeking to live the American dream free of government interference. They believe themselves to be right, and they believe that terrorism is necessary in a war against evil. How are they different from those nations defined as an "axis of evil"? Does our willingness to resort to this invidious distinction reflect our inability to see or accept the linkage between us and them? If so, how can we hope to change them or ourselves? Can we as a nation insist that, say, blacks or Native Americans forget and forgive the atrocities visited upon them, yet refuse to embrace a similar "paradox of healing" toward external attackers?

"Training for Uncertainty" and Identity Politics

Thinking about my own life—my struggle for space to be me and to flourish as me—I confront the white male identity struggle as a fellow traveler. That is, I see matters of difference, development, and secure vulnerability as paramount. I will illustrate what I am feeling with a story.

A few nights back, I stopped in my neighborhood bar. It was a rainy Sunday evening. The bar was nearly empty. I was sitting to the side, watching Tiger Woods win another match and editing this book. The bar maid, a middle-aged lady, was chatting with two other patrons who were also her good friends. The conversation wandered here and there, about this and that. At one point, the women became very animated, talking about raising sons and daughters and being grandmothers. One woman began telling a story of how her youngest son, a thirty-year-old bachelor who still lived at home with her and his father, had been scratched in the face by his girlfriend. She was very upset with this young woman and expressed a desire to let her know that "I have raised my sons to not touch a woman physically. . . . I don't expect a woman to hit him even though he is a grown man because I raised him to not ever hit a woman regardless of the reason."

There were many nuances in this particular conversation that I found intriguing. The one that struck me most—and clearly the one of greatest significance to these black mothers—was the particular vulnerability of their sons to women when trained to be nonaggressive or nonretaliatory toward women aggressors. These mothers seemed anxious because they, as black women, had insisted that their sons be different from most other men and not protect themselves against female abuse.

It is precisely this absence of "identity armor" that many white males I have spoken with describe when discussing women and nonwhite males. Specifically, they mention the isolation, the sense of being uncertain about where they fit. My friend Robert beautifully described just this emotionality in chapter 3 in a passage from his semiautobiographical work:

> When a person lives psychologically outside of his culture to a considerable degree for a sufficient period of time, and being told that he should be like everyone else, he begins to question his own sanity; he must be crazy. I had these feelings as a child. I made a vow I would not go crazy. There were times when I thought I was going crazy. During those times, I would beat my fist against the wall, breathe deeply, sing to myself, rock furiously in a rocking chair radio up loud and concentrate on each word. I was, in fact, having what is called a panic attack. ACOAs may have more than their share of these. (Haskell 1993: 103–4)

Robert is here attributing his emotions to being an adult child of an alcoholic mother. These emotions are also often present in other situations, including those characterized by uncertainty of who one is vis-à-vis others, how one stands, and what one should or should not do or say. A student recently wrote in an autobiographical essay that her interactions with her estranged father were characterized by this same kind of uncertainty. Because her mother and father tell different stories of the family breakup, she asked,

> With my dad, I wonder if my brothers or I are ever really happy and comfortable . . . you have to beware what you say for fear you step on his toes by doing or saying something that even though it matters little to us, my dad finds a way to take offense . . . We are always on edge around him, trying to be the angel kids that we are not.

The need for a *secured vulnerability* is critical to healthy existence. Some psychologists, especially those concerned with the development of healthy, autonomous individuals and citizens, have described this condition as "object constancy" (Blanck and Blanck 1979). It is that point emotionally at which people do not come undone because of the disappointments or assaults to their ego that go with life. For example, a man loses his mate to another, grieves for while, then picks himself up and goes on; a woman loses a job and makes the necessary adjustments personally and professionally to find another position. To reach this point, people must have been raised to believe that they are OK even if they are not at the center of the universe, even if they are not always affirmed. This is an important theme in the emerging literature on whiteness. For example, Becky Thompson, associate professor at Simmons College, wrote for the *Boston Globe* in 1997: "What I've learned in 10 years of teaching about race identity is how to experience a much richer life than I was born into." She goes on to say that, increasingly, white Americans will be finding out that "you don't have to be the center of the universe to be part of the universe" (John Yemma, "'Whiteness Studies,' an Attempt at Healing," *Boston Globe Online*, December 21, 1997).

What is important here is finding a balance between the propensities for *self-display* that Michael Apple attributes to whites and, far less likely but nonetheless deadly, for escape into destructive self-negation.

Michelle Fine wrote just a few years ago:

With the generosity of a Spencer Foundation grant, Lois Weis and I, with our graduate students, have been conducting interviews in Jersey City and Buffalo with white, African American, Latino, and Asian young adults—age twenty-one to twenty-nine—poor and working class. In one slice of this project we have collected oral histories from white working-class men, narrating, in part, their current economic plight. By listening to these "angry white men" one can hear how global flight of capital and the consequential labor-market scarcity has sharpened and prolonged racial identities, tensions, and sedimentation. While relative to their fathers these white working-class men have taken a disproportional hit under the macroeconomic policies of Reagan and Bush, the flight of capital out of the Northeast and out of the country, and the dismantling of blue collar unions, these men, when interviewed, lay blame for their economic woes squarely at the feet of African American males. Not Republicans, not global capitalists, not elites. African American men . . . are discursively imported to buffer the pain, protest the loss, and still secure the artificial privilege of whiteness. (1997: 62)

Fine's observations are critical to our conversation because she locates loss of illusion as a source for pain among less privileged white males. This is a real issue for anti-oppression activists, even though black males have long endured, and continue to endure, precisely this dislocation. It is, in part, this loss that many feel to underlay much machismo and male self-destruction among certain classes of minority men. An interesting alternative message issues from some white men: minorities should view them in a different way than they have previously. This is a call for the recognition of white male heterogeneity and changeability. An impasse is implicit in the insistence that women and minorities change, too. It is important to recognize that white males like those interviewed by Fine and her colleagues must have "functional" alternatives to the "privileges of whiteness" if change is to be successful. One aspect of an alternative identity is recognition by the other as a growing being. To be sure, there is a certain irony and immaturity in this need. Thompson (1999) has called this the need for whites to be recognized as "good people" for doing the right thing. She is correct, I believe, in suggesting that this expectation must be overcome. Still, some form of recognition by the other does seem to be essential. I can only return to the image of Mandela's donning the Afrikaner's football jersey, even though he had been the injured one. The gesture—turning the other cheek, going the extra mile—is necessary for healing among unequals, maybe even for equals. But it cannot be the final resolution to the power imbalance.

Conclusion

Apartheid was abolished in South Africa in the early 1990s. "White rule" was at an end. Blacks assumed a greater political and social primacy, and whites were induced to participate in a dance of guilt as part of a national drama of contrition and reconciliation. Around the country, nightly television programs portrayed whites soliloquizing on their complicity in the country's racist legacy and reign of tyranny. Mandela's government had inaugurated these public hearings in July 1995 as part of the National Unity and Reconciliation Act.

According to Bishop Desmond Tutu, head of the Truth and Reconciliation Commission, the practical justification for the Reconciliation Act was to protect the new multicultural democracy by appeasing powerful and well-armed whites. This unfolding story reminds us of both similarities and differences between South Africa and the United States. Mandela's South Africa, like Lincoln's country, had to find a way of replacing racist ideology and national policy and practice with a vision of suffrage for all. Each had to grapple with the democratic implications of one vote for one citizen, and both accomplished this end more or less.

But the United States is not South Africa on many dimensions. The meaning of race and its centrality to white American identity is one of these dimensions, which is central also to the meaning and operation of race in the contemporary and emergent discourse on diversity. This discourse ranges from traditional affirmative action policy debates to diversity in the workplace and the more recent "racial profiling" of potential terrorists. Racial identity, especially for white males, is linked to both manhood and socioeconomic placement. Changes in both the understanding of masculinity (Bederman 1995) and the political economic infrastructure threaten the dominant white male self-understanding. Moreover, the very structure of much multiculturalism activity has an aspect of character assassination that must be addressed differently now than in the past.

At present, South Africa is working through its dialectical heritage. In the United States, the various liberation efforts of the past three decades also have been churning along toward some form of stasis. But the South African and American struggles for racial equality are very different species of human struggle. In the United States, the concession to racial minorities was and remains an accommodation. It is because this adjustment was largely symbolic and involved verbal and visual strategies that compromised traditional white self-other understandings that recovery and atonement are necessary (Gresson 1995). Unfortunately, there is a deep-rooted problem here. In his brilliant *Regeneration through Violence*, Richard Slotkin (1973) opens with an epigraph from D. H. Lawrence's *Studies in Classic American Literature:*

> But you have there the myth of the essential white America. All the other stuff, the love, the democracy, the floundering into lust, is a sort of by-play. The essential American soul is hard, isolate, stoic, and a killer. It has never yet melted.

There is much about this depiction that might be challenged, and rightly so. Chief among the challenges might be the fact that the country is becoming increasingly less white and more diverse. In addition, the classic discussion of black and white itself is becoming more problematic. Other groups have increased both their power and visibility and have revealed as well "the essential American soul." There is no doubt that the old ways of seeing Us/Them are changing, and the future complexion and composition of the country have yet to be clarified. But it is precisely this cultural and social change that calls forth a prior "American soul," one constituted through myths and histories that continue to be used in the struggle to retain some of the traditional image of a "white" self.

Recent discussions of white youth identification with hip-hop culture as well as the reemployment of blackface by white college students point to this struggle. As such identity fluxes play out on the societal landscape, we are reminded that this entire process has a strong history:

> The mythopoeic mode of reconciling historical paradoxes enables us to glory in this role, on the one hand, and to take the curse off our axe- and gun-work, on the other, by allowing us to identify with what is wounded or destroyed. In the captivity myth, the unfilial emigrant is reconciled with his family by identification with the suffering of the female captive and by his recognition that his masculine will to achieve in the wilderness world is the true cause of her suffering. But the vicarious suffering obtained through the captivity myth atones for the sin and permits the continuance of the emigrant's career. (Slotkin 1973: 563)

Slotkin is describing here how the mythology of the American frontier enabled the "winning of the West." Significant in his description is the belief that sins can be atoned for through vicarious identification with the vulnerable and the vanquished. Some writers have described this process as cannibalism, but it is perhaps best understood in the contemporary context by notions such as "white male as victim of affirmative action," "reverse racism," and "black racism." The rise of the notion of "white power" symbolizes this process of atonement and the convoluted logic underpinning these other metaphors. This term signals the nature of the "new racism," which is largely semiotic or sign-based, employing the mass media to convey the "bullets" that "kill" imagination and intellect.

The second Iraq War of 2003 also echoes the phantasm of atonement-seeking described by Slotkin. The words attributed to Sadaam Hussein, on the eve of his destruction, seem uncannily relevant: "They thought that they would be able to heal their wounds if they went against Baghdad." Should we be surprised that an evil tyrant recognizes a traditional modus operandi? Have we not, at least in part, continued our conqueror's career in Iraq even as we claim sinlessness and atonement for past sins? If not, how do we explain the repeated insistence that the American flag be raised in Baghdad, or that the soldier who displayed the Stars and Stripes about the statue of Sadaam Hussein confessed he was "just following orders"?

These questions have yet to be answered. But we are moved to ask them, and perhaps that best instructs us in the continuing dialectics of social pain and collective healing.

EPILOGUE

CONVERSATION IN A BLACK BAR

Pain Begets Pain When Identity Is Threatened

My answer is not right or wrong. It's your opinion [that's wrong].
BLACK WOMAN, MARCH 15, 2002

Last Friday night I stopped in a neighborhood bar to have a drink and unwind with the fellows—middle-aged, middle-class black men. As is often the case, the conversation turned to racism. One man, a retired city policeman, was venting his rage at white America. Another, a senior administrator at an urban high school, was chiding his lifelong friend because he knew this man was generally an even-tempered, solid citizen. However, another brother was very upset with the conversation's seemingly anti-American tone. Eventually, the battle came to that point familiar to many African Americans when we're challenged with the question: Are you an American or an African?

Of course, this generally leads to an affirmation: we love America, racism notwithstanding. When that night's "antagonist"—for in truth, we all have found ourselves in the role of "revolutionary African warrior"—proceeded to call us "Uncle Toms," the younger brother, a Vietnam veteran with a strong military-patriotic persona, left the group and approached a woman selecting songs at the nearby jukebox. He asked her how she felt about September 11 and our soldiers in Afghanistan. She took his question well, even though he had intruded into her own entertainment and group space (she had two other black women waiting for her at the bar). She answered, "I feel something in my heart for the people who were killed; I hurt for them and their families. But I wouldn't want my children over there. I don't think we should be over there."

To this response, with strong emotion and self-righteousness, the brother-soldier declared her unpatriotic and her answer as "wrong." Now showing her own emotion, she replied with the words opening this epilogue.

I relate this little drama because it helps illustrate just how convoluted and comprehensive the issues are that have been discussed in *America's Atonement*. In particular, these two people indicate the vast gulf that may separate people, even those of the same race, class, and sociopolitical circumstances. Furthermore, the story illustrates how personal identity and subjective perspective are tied up with what we say about the world and how we choose to comport ourselves in it. Most of all, we see how a threatened identity can lead people to talk past each other and to cause pain in the process.

In looking back over this book, I am struck with how mundane the points are that I wish to make. I have said very little that is new or unfamiliar or unimaginable. Still, I believe that the ideas presented here must be repeatedly offered to others for their reflection, rejection, and, when expedient and feasible, their adoption and action. This seems to me to be the pathos of the kind of revolutionary change confronting the country and the world. I see it in the unfolding Israeli-Palestinian dance of agency. The escalating war and devastating loss of life there is a mere sidebar to the drama all seemed prepared to play out. Everyone knows Israel must exist, but the Palestinians also should be permitted to have an independent state. Few people disagree. But not enough blood has been sacrificed, and so as this "bloody sacrifice" unfolds, we wait.

This seems to be the human condition. Again, I can state only the obvious. Nonetheless, there is hope that this kind of activity will quicken the spirits and passions of more and more people until we outnumber those who have no fear of the gods or of the void. Only then, perhaps, will the choice to embrace the otherness in both ourselves and others prevail.

Rejection of the inevitability of finitude seems to be at the base of much human destructiveness. It is as if the refusal to admit that we are indeed but one among many stays the necessity of ordinary existence: struggle, suffering, insignificance. So we try to grasp the sublime, the supra, and designate ourselves other than "the other." In this way, we are freed to feed on "the ordinary." It is, in part, this rejection of the ordinary that Jean-Paul Sartre attributes to the "hunter" in his *Anti-Semite and Jew:*

The Jew is only a pretext, elsewhere it will be the Negro, the yellow race. The Jew's insistence simply allows the anti-semite to nip his anxieties in the bud by persuading himself that his place has always been cut out in the world, that it was waiting for him and by virtue of tradition he has the right to occupy it. *Anti-semitism*, in a word, *is fear of man's fate.* The anti-semite is the man who wants to be pitiless stone, furious torrent, devastating lightning: in short, everything but a man. (cited in McWilliams 1948: 268)

These are powerful thoughts. Meditating on them may help remind us of the future challenge, whether multiracial, multicultural, or monolithically homogenous. Change and growth are essential, but they are not guaranteed. Rejecting the necessity of change, especially in matters of identity, while understandable, portends a great concern for the future.

In recent months, two new conversations have surfaced on the diversity circuit: "white diversity leadership" and "emotional intelligence." The first, discussed briefly in chapter 5, stands as an opportunity for whites to join "the other" in transforming the world community. It is important, indeed, for whites to acknowledge white privilege and to share in its dismantling when it is indicated. But we must recall Michael Apple's (1998) exhortation that the white person's propensity for "self-display" should not be indulged further than it has already.

"Emotional intelligence" is a fairly new concept (Gardner 1993; Goleman 1995). Its significance for the discussion of white pain is equally interesting as that of white diversity leadership, again if it does not degenerate into pop self-indulgence. What is perhaps most important about this growing cluster of fields is the futuristic reach for an evolutionary leap within the species that may push us beyond the quagmire of human destructiveness so far dominating the world. The impulse itself is not a new one, but the urgency—including apocalyptic crises that presumably will follow further global warming—may be part of the equation needed to push the impulse to the next level.

I mention these themes in this epilogue because they may represent the most persuasive "secular" initiatives currently focused on the twin issues of privilege and pain taken up in this book. For the moment, we have largely stepped away from racism per se and turned our collective sights on global stability and continued global economic development/exploitation. By reframing diversity matters in business terms (see http://equ.org.busi.htm) and viewing them through an economic lens, some attention has been taken away from racial blame without necessarily abrogating the awareness of and responsibility for continued, systemic changes in this area. It is certainly my hope that racial pain, as a subspecies of human pain, can be ameliorated through greater attention to the emotional life of Americans. And perhaps a refocusing on "emotional intelligence" can aid this process. If not, then more pain is in our collective future.

NOTES

Preface

1. See *The Chronicle of Higher Education*, January 5, January 19, and April 26, 1996. These news features cover the charges against the University of Minnesota Press, the racial divide at the university presses, and the dismissal of charges against the then director of the university press. Although Biodun Iginla, the Nigeria-born former senior editor, planned to file a civil suit against Ms Lisa Freeman, the university, and the press, nothing was subsequently reported about this.

Introduction

1. For one of the most profound statements on this topic as it applies to contemporary society, see Eli Sagan, *Cannibalism: Human Aggression and Cultural Form* (New York: Harper & Row, 1974).

Chapter 2

1. "Tutu and Franklin: A Journey towards Peace," PBS, February 9, 2001. See www.pbs.org/journeytopeace/thedoc/.

Chapter 4

1. The classic discussion of master-slave has rountinely inferred a shared fate, a complementary bond. This discussion focused largely on the fact that both master and slave lose some portion of their humanity in the enslavement process. Later thinkers, such as Gramsci, seem to retain this complemetary bond. Hence Gramsci defines "hegemony" as a collusion between the more and less powerful

around some shared investment, even though the less powerful are effectively enabling and abetting their own domination.

Chapter 5

1. This statement is not intended to suggest that every one equally or significantly participates in oppressive identification. Clearly, people choose different available "materials" for forging their individual identities. Nonetheless, people are social entities and operate more or less within the sociocultural parameters dominating their society.

2. The great "positivist, scientific" experiment, of which the academy is an example, has a fraudulent feature: it assumes that what goes on in the classroom has a motive different from that of public propaganda. But this is untrue when we try to implement a "human science" with both moral authority and technical competence. The "logic" of the classroom is an assumption that we can "air" our differences without damaging our selves. This also is not true. In chapter 4, I discussed the work of Stanton Wortham (1994), who describes how the use of certain examples in the classroom can lead to extraclass partisanship. That is, what goes on in the classroom can deepen rather than loosen problematic perspectives and values. Of course, more recent work on pedagogies of antiracism and nonoppression (Butin 2002) pushes the point even further.

3. Again, we see the dialectic at work. This surrender to and identification with the other has been called "identification with the aggressor" when undertaken by the less powerful in relation to the more powerful. Self-hate is a popular way of identifying this behavior that seems conciliatory (Gresson 1982). The recent suggestion that whites calling for the elimination of "whiteness" are self-hating rather than "nonracist" is related to this "identification with the aggressor" theme. Thus we see that healing is dialectic and only partly fulfills the "wholeness" metaphor it implies.

4. *Fiddler on the Roof* was a 1964 Broadway musical based on the short story "Tevye and His Daughters" by Sholom Aleichem. Set in 1905, *Fiddler on the Roof* takes place in Anatevka, a small Jewish village in Russia. The story revolves around a dairyman, Tevye, and his attempts to preserve his family's traditions in the face of a changing world. The term "fiddler on a roof" is a metaphor for the life of Jews in the Diaspora. At a critical point in the play, Tevye says that life for the Jew is very much like a fiddler trying to keep his balance on a roof, that this balancing act is possible only because of "tradition." Because of tradition, each Jew knows who he is and what God expects him to do; this is the secret to survival. It has been argued that the universal appeal of the ploy in this play/movie is the reason for its monumental success, even though such works usually fail on Broadway.

5. Rabbi Jonathan Sacks, chief rabbi of Britain and the Commonwealth ("The Hatred That Won't Die," *The Guardian*, February 28, 2002, www.guardian.co.uk), writes regarding anti-Semitism, notably the murder in Pakistan of the American journalist Daniel Pearl: "He is shown being forced to kneel and confess that he and his parents are Jewish. His throat is then cut. Over his writhing body, a voice warns: 'Americans and Jews should be ready to face a fate like Pearl.'" The struggle

to break with being defined by one's otherness is pervasive. Then again, some Jews see anti-Semitism as part of Jewish identity. So did Jean-Paul Sartre, who claimed in his "Sur le question juif" that the only thing Jews had in common was that they were the victims of hate. It is not Jews who create anti-Semitism, he said, but anti-Semitism that creates Jews. I have fought that view all my adult life. It leads to the tortured psychology of Arthur Koestler, who wrote: "Self-hatred is the Jews' patriotism," or Franz Kafka, who said: "What do I have in common with the Jews? I don't even have anything in common with myself." To me, Jewishness is about moral responsibility, not victimhood; about trust, not fear. Anti-Semitism is something that happens to Jews; it does not define who we are.

REFERENCES

Allison, Clinton B. 1995. *Present and Past: Essays for Teachers in the History of Education.* New York: Peter Lang.

Allmendinger, Black. 1992. *The Cowboy: Representations of Labor in an American Work Culture.* New York: Oxford University Press.

Alridge, Derrick P. 2001. "Redefining and Refining Scholarship for the Academy: Standing on the Shoulders of Our Elders and Giving Credence to African-American Voice and Agency." In *Retaining African Americans in Higher Education: Challenging Paradigms for Retaining Students, Faculty & Administrators,* edited by Lee Jones. Sterling, Va.: Stylus.

Anyon, J. 1995. "Race, Social Class, and Educational Reform in an Inner-city School." *Teachers College Record* 97 (Fall): 69–94.

Apple, Michael W. 1993. "Constructing the 'Other': Rightist Reconstruction of Common Sense." In *Race Identity and Representation in Education,* edited by Cameron McCarthy and Warren Crichlow. New York: Routledge.

———. 1998. Foreword to *White Reign: Deploying Whiteness in America,* edited by Joe L. Kincheloe et al. New York: St. Martin's Press.

Aronowitz, S. 1992. *The Politics of Identity: Class, Culture, Social Movements.* New York: Routledge.

Asante, Molefi. 1988. *Afrocentricity.* New Brunswick, N.J.: African World Press.

Asante, M. K. and D. Atwater. 1986. "The Rhetorical Condition as Symbolic Structure in Discourse." *Communication Quarterly* 34 (Spring): 170–77.

Atkinson, William. 2001. "Bringing Diversity to White Men." *HR Magazine,* September Online: www.findarticles.com.

Bakhtin, M. M. 1986. *The Dialogic Imagination.* Austin: University of Texas Press.

Banks, James A., ed. 1981. *Education in the 80's: Multiethnic Education.* Washington, D.C.: National Education Association.

Banks, James A., and Cherry A. McGee Banks, eds. 1989. *Multicultural Education: Issues and Perspectives.* Boston: Allyn & Bacon.

Barthes, Roland. 1972. *Mythologies.* Translated by Annette Lavers. London: Granada.

Bederman, Gail. 1995. *Manliness and Civilization: A Cultural History of Gender and Race in the United States, 1880–1917.* Chicago: University of Chicago Press.

Beers, William. 1992. *Women and Sacrifice: Male Narcissism and the Psychology of Religion.* Detroit: Wayne State University Press.

Bell, Terel H. 1986. "Education Policy Development in the Reagan Administration." *Phi Delta Kappan* 67 (March): 487–93.

Bennett, Christine I. 1990. *Comprehensive Multicultural Education Theory and Practice.* Boston: Allyn & Bacon.

Berger-Knorr, Ann L. 1997. "Unlearning Privilege: Gender, Race, and Class in Reading Methods." Ph.D. diss., Pennsylvania State University.

Berlak, Ann C. 1990. "Experiencing Teaching: Viewing and Re-viewing Education." Paper presented at the annual meeting of the American Education Research Association, Boston.

———. 1996. "Teaching Stories: Viewing a Cultural Diversity Course through the Lens of Narrative." *Theory into Practice* 35: 93–101.

Berliner, Michael S., and Gary Hull. 1996. "Diversity and Multiculturalism." Marina del Rey, Calif.: Ayn Rand Institute / Center for the Advancement of Objectivism.

Bettleheim, Bruno. 1962. *Symbolic Wounds: Puberty Rites and the Envious Male.* 2d ed. New York: Collier.

Blanck, Gertrude, and Rubin Blanck. 1979. *Ego Psychology II.* New York: Columbia University Press.

Blee, Kathleen M. 1991. *Women of the Klan: Racism and Gender in the 1920s.* Berkeley and Los Angeles: University of California Press.

Blum, Debra E. 1991. "Faculty Notes: White Male Professor Sues Black Women's College." *Chronicle of Higher Education*, May 29, A12.

Bollin, G. G., and J. Finkel. 1995. "White racial identity as a barrier to understanding diversity: A study of preservice teachers." *Equity & Excellence in Education*, 28(1): 25–30.

Bork, Robert H. 1996. *Slouching towards Gomorrah: Modern Liberalism and American Decline.* New York: Regan Books.

Bowen, Murray. 1985. *Family Therapy in Clinical Practice.* New York: Jason Aronson.

Breen, Michael Daniel. 1965. "Culture and Schizophrenia: A Study of Negro and Jewish Schizophrenics." Ph.D. diss., Brandeis University.

Britzman, Deborah P. 1991. "The Terrible Problem of Knowing Thyself: Toward a Poststructural Account of Teacher Identity." *Journal of Curriculum Theorizing* 9: 22–46.

Britzman, Deborah P., and Alice J. Pitt. 1996. "Pedagogy and Transference: Casting the Past of Learning into the Presence of Teaching." *Theory into Practice* 35: 117–23.

Brown, Norman O. 1966. *Love's Body.* New York: Vintage Books.

Butin, D. 2002. "If This Is Resistance I Would Hate to See Domination: Retrieving Foucault's Notion of Resistance within Educational Research." *Educational Studies* 32: 157–76.

Carby, Hazel. 1993. "Encoding White Resentment: Grand Canyon—A Narrative for Our Times." In *Race Identity and Representation in Education*, edited by Cameron McCarthy and Warren Crichlow. New York: Routledge.

Chapman, Dan, Bob Deans, and Craig Nelson. 2003. "War in the Gulf: Special Coverage: U.S. trails in battle for world opinion." ajc.com, Sunday, March 30.

Chennault, Ronald E. 1998. "Race, Reagan, Education, and Cinema: Hollywood Films about Schools in the 1980s and 1990s." Ph.D. diss., Pennsylvania State University.

Corliss, Richard. 1994. "The World according to Gump." *Time*, August 1: 52–54.

Corti, Carlo. 2002. "Finding Myself in My Students: A Step Toward Transforming Social Dynamics in the Classroom." In *Learning to Teach for Social Justice*, edited by Linda Darling-Hammond, Jennifer French, and Silvia Paloma Garcia-Lopez. New York: Teachers College Press: 52–65.

Crosby, F. J. 1997. "Confessions of an Affirmative Action Mama." In *Off White: Readings on Race, Power and Society*, edited by Michelle Fine et al. New York: Routledge.

Dalton, Harlon L. 1996. *Racial Healing: Confronting the Fear between Blacks and Whites*. New York: Doubleday/Anchor.

Daly, Mary. 1978. *Gyn/Ecology: The Metaethics of Radical Feminism*. Boston: Beacon Press.

Darling-Hammond, Linda, Jennifer French, and Silvia Paloma Garcia-Lopez, eds. 2002. *Learning to Teach for Social Justice*. New York: Teachers College Press.

DeSousa, Michael A. 1984. "Symbolic Action and Pretended Insight: The Ayatollah Khomeini in U.S. Editorial Cartoons." In *Rhetorical Dimensions in Media: A Critical Casebook*, edited by Martin J. Medhurst and Thomas W. Benson. Dubuque, Iowa: Kendall/Hunt: 204–30.

Dickar, Maryann. 1999. "Teaching in Our Underwear: The Liabilities of Whiteness in the Multi-Racial Classroom." *William and Mary College Researcher* 11: 1–22.

Dilg, Mary. 1999. *Race and Culture in the Classroom: Teaching and Learning through Multicultural Education*. New York: Teachers College Press.

Dillard, Cynthia B. 1996. "Engaging Pedagogy: Writing and Reflecting in Multicultural Teacher Education." *Teaching Education* 8: 13–21.

Dinnerstein, Dorothy. 1976. *The Mermaid and the Minotaur: Sexual Arrangements and Human Malaise*. New York: HarperCollins.

Doane, Janice, and Devon Hodges. 1987. *Nostalgia and Sexual Difference: The Resistance to Contemporary Feminism*. New York: Methuen.

D'Souza, Dinesh. 1995. *The End of Racism: Principles for a Multicultural Society*. New York: Free Press.

Dumas, R. G. 1980. "Dilemmas of Black Females in Leadership." In *The Black Woman*, edited by L. Rodgers-Rose. Beverly Hills, Calif.: Sage.

Dziech, Billie Wright. 1995. "Coping with the Alienation of White Male Students." *Chronicle of Higher Education* January: B1–2.

Ellsworth, E. 1989. "Why Doesn't This Feel Empowering? Working through the Repressive Myth of Critical Pedagogy." *Harvard Education Review* 59: 297–324.

Faludi, Susan. 1992. *Backlash: The Undeclared War against American Women*. New York: Anchor Books.

Fanon, Franz. 1967. *Black Skin, White Masks*. New York: Grove Press.

———. 1968. *The Wretched of the Earth*. New York: Grove Press.

Feagin, Joe R., and Hernan Vera. 2001. *White Racism: The Basics*. 2d ed. New York: Routledge.

Fine, Michelle. 1997. "Witnessing White." In *Off White: Readings on Race, Power and Society*, edited by Michelle Fine et al. New York: Routledge.

Fiske, John. 1994. *Media Matters: Everyday Culture and Political Change*. Minneapolis: University of Minnesota Press.

———. 1993. *Power plays, power works*. New York: Verso.

Foster, Peter. 1990. *Policy and Practice in Multicultural and Anti-Racist Education*. London: Routledge.

Foucault, M. 1977. *Discipline and Punishment: The Birth of the Prison*. New York: Vintage Books.

———. 1978. *The History of Sexuality*. Vol. 1, An Introduction. New York: Vintage Books.

Frankenberg, Ruth. 1993. *White Women, Race Matters: The Social Construction of Whiteness*. Minneapolis: University of Minnesota Press.

Freire, Paulo. 1970. *Pedagogy of the Oppressed*, translated by M. B. Ramos. New York: Continuum.

Freire, Paulo, et al., eds. 1997. *Mentoring the Mentor: A Critical Dialogue with Paulo Freire*. New York: Peter Lang.

French, Jennifer. 2002. "Idealism Meets Reality." In *Learning to Teach for Social Justice*, edited by Linda Darling-Hammond, Jennifer French, and Silvia Paloma Garcia-Lopez. New York: Teachers College Press: 59–70.

Gardner, H. 1993. *Multiple Intelligences*. New York: Basic Books.

Gardner, S., C. Dean, and D. McKaig. 1989. "Responding to Difference in the Classroom: The Politics of Knowledge, Class, and Sexuality." *Sociology of Education* 62: 64–74.

Gee, J. 1992. *The Social Mind*. Westport, Conn.: Greenwood Press.

Gerzon, Mark. 1982. *A Choice of Heroes: The Changing Face of American Manhood*. Boston: Houghton Mifflin.

Gibbs, Nancy. 1995. "The EQ Factor: New Brain Research Suggests That Emotions, Not I.Q., May Be the True Measure of Human Intelligence." *Time* 146 (14), October 2: 60–69.

Gilbert, Sandra M. 1989. "Soldier's Heart: Literary Men, Literary Women, and the Great War." In *Speaking of Gender*, edited by Elaine Showalter. New York: Routledge.

Ginsburg, Mark B. 1988. *Contradictions in Teacher Education and Society : A Critical Analysis*. New York: Falmer Press.

Giroux, Henry A. 1995. "Who Writes in a Cultural Studies Class: Or, Where Is the Pedagogy?" In *Left Margins: Cultural Studies and Composition Pedagogy*, edited by Karen Fitts and Alan W. France. Albany: State University of New York Press.

———. 1997. *Pedagogy and the Politics of Hope: Theory, Culture, and Schooling*. Boulder, Colo.: Westview Press.

———. 1998. *Channel surfing: Racism, the Media and the Destruction of Today's Youth*. New York: St. Martin's Press.

Goffman, Erving. 1963. *Stigma: Notes on the Management of Spoiled Identity*. Englewood Cliffs, N.J.: Prentice-Hall.

Goldberg, David Theo, ed. 1990. *Anatomy of Racism*. Minneapolis: University of Minnesota Press.

Goleman, D. 1995. *Emotional Intelligence*. New York: Bantam Books.

Goodman, J. 1988. "Constructing a Practical Philosophy of Teaching: A Study of Preservice Teachers' Professional Perspectives." *Teaching and Teacher Education* 4: 121–37.

Goodwin, L. 1997. "Multicultural Stories: Preservice Teacher's Conceptions of and Responses to Issues of Diversity." *Urban Education* 32: 117–45.

Gore, Jennifer. 1993. *The Struggle for Pedagogies: Critical Feminist Discourses as Regimes of Truth*. New York: Routledge.

Grant, C. 1994. "Best Practices in Teacher Preparation for Urban Schools: Lessons from the Multicultural Teacher Education Literature." *Action in Teacher Education* 16: 1–18.

Gresson, Aaron David III. 1976. "Non-negotiables and Academic Activist." *Black Sociologist* 5: 4–6.

———. 1977. "Minority Epistemology and the Rhetoric of Creation." *Philosophy and Rhetoric* 10: 244–62.

———. 1978. "Phenomenology and the Rhetoric of Identification: A Neglected Dimension of Coalition Communication." *Communication Quarterly* 26: 14–23.

———. 1982. *The Dialectics of Betrayal: Sacrifice, Violation and the Oppressed.* Norwood, N.J.: Ablex.

———. 1987. "Transitional Metaphors and the Political Psychology of Identity Maintenance." In *Cognition and Symbolic Structures: The Psychology of Metaphoric Transformations,* edited by Robert E. Haskell. Norwood, N.J.: Ablex.

———. 1989. "Equity and Excellence among Ethnic Groups: Toward the Transcendence of Self-Deception." In *Excellence and Equity—A Reassessment,* edited by David G. Carter and J. John Harris III. Bloomington: Indiana University Press.

———. 1990. *Black Amnesia.* Baltimore: Transformation Books.

———. 1995. *The Recovery of Race in America.* Minneapolis: University of Minnesota Press.

———. 1996a. "Coda: Relational Justice and the Cognitive Elite." In *Measured Lies: The Bell Curve Examined,* edited by Joe L. Kincheloe, Shirley R. Steinberg, and Aaron D. Gresson III. New York: St. Martin's Press.

———. 1996b. "Postmodern America and the Multiculturalism Crisis: Reading Forrest Gump as the 'Call Back to Whiteness.'" *Taboo* 2: 11–33.

———. 1997. "Identity, Class, and Teacher Education: The Persistence of 'Class Effects' in the Classroom." *Review of Education/Pedagogy/Cultural Studies* 19: 348–56.

———. 2000. Foreword to *Dismantling White Privilege: Pedagogy, Politics, and Whiteness,* edited by Nelson M. Rodriquez and Leila Villaverde. New York: Peter Lang.

Haines, Harry W. 1986. "What Kind of War? An Analysis of the Vietnam Veterans Memorial." *Critical Studies in Mass Communication* 3: 1–17.

Harris, Jeffrey Donald. 1986. "The Rhetoric of the Vietnam Veterans Memorial: An Analysis of News Magazine and Network Television News Coverage." M.A. thesis, Pennsylvania State University.

Harper, H., and S. Cavenaugh. 1994. "Lady Bountiful: The White Woman Teacher in Multicultural Education." *Women's Education* 11: 27–33.

Haskell, Robert E. 1987. *Cognition and Symbolic Structures: The Psychology of Metaphoric Transformations.* Norwood, N.J.: Ablex.

———. 1993. *Adult-Child Research and Experience: Personal and Professional Legacies of a Dysfunctional, Co-Dependent Family.* Norwood, N.J.: Ablex.

Hedley, Mark. 1994. "The Presentation of Gendered Conflict in Popular Movies: Affective Stereotypes, Cultural Sentiments, and Men's Motivations." *Sex Roles,* December, 721–40.

Heinemann, Larry. 1986. *Paco's Story.* New York : Farrar, Straus & Giroux.

Hill, Alette. 1984. "The Carter Campaign in Retrospect: Decoding the Cartoons." In *Rhetorical Dimensions in Media: A Critical Casebook,* edited by Martin J. Medhurst and Thomas W. Benson. Dubuque, Iowa: Kendall/Hunt Publishing.

Hinson, Hal. 1994. "Forrest Gump, Our National Folk Zero." *Washington Post,* August 14, G1:1.

Homans, Peter. 1989. *The Ability to Mourn: Disillusionment and the Social Origins of Psychoanalysis.* Chicago: University of Chicago Press.

hooks, bell. 1994. *Teaching to Transgress: Education as the Practice of Freedom.* New York: Routledge.

Horrocks, Roger. 1994. *Masculinity in Crisis: Myths, Fantasies and Realities.* New York: St. Martin's Press.

————. 1995. *Male Myths and Icons: Masculinity in Popular Culture*. New York: St. Martin's Press.

Hull, G., P. Scott, and B. Smith. 1982. *All of the Women Are White, All of the Blacks Are Men, but Some of Us Are Brave: Black Women's Studies*. Old Westbury, New York: Feminist Press.

Ipsaro, Anthony J. 1997. *White Men, Women and Minorities in the Changing Work Force*. Denver: Meridian Associates.

Isaacs, Harold R. 1975. *Idols of the Tribe: Group Identity and Political Change*. New York: Harper & Row.

Jacoby, Russell. 1975. *Social Amnesia: A Critique of Contemporary Psychology from Adler to Laing*. Boston: Beacon Press.

Jeffords, Susan. 1989. *The Remasculinization of America: Gender and the Vietnam War*. Bloomington: Indiana University Press.

————. 1994. *Hard Bodies: Hollywood Masculinity in the Reagan Era*. New Brunswick, N.J.: Rutgers University Press.

Jewel, K. Sue. 1993. *From Mammy to Miss America and Beyond: Images and the Shaping of U.S. Social Policy*. New York: Routledge.

Kadish, Doris Y. 1991. *Politicizing Gender: Narrative Strategies in the Aftermath of the French Revolution*. New Brunswick, N.J.: Rutgers University Press.

Kanpol, Barry. 1997. "Critical Pedagogy for Beginning Teachers: The Movement from Despair to Hope." *Journal of Critical Pedagogy* 2: 1.

Kanpol, Barry, and Jeanne Brady. 1997. "Teacher Education and the Multicultural Dilemma: A 'Critical' Thinking Response." *Journal of Critical Pedagogy* 1: 1–17.

Kaufmann, Stanley. 1994. "Different." *New Republic*, August 8: 28–29.

Kellner, Douglas. 1991. "Reading Images Critically: Toward a Postmodern Pedagogy." In *Postmodernism, Feminism, and Cultural Politics: Redrawing Educational Boundaries*, edited by Henry Giroux. Albany: State University of New York Press.

Kimmel, Michael S., and Michael A. Messner, eds. 2001. *Men's Lives*. 5th Ed. Boston: Allyn and Bacon.

Kincheloe, Joe L. 1999. "The Struggle to Define and Reinvent Whiteness: A Pedagogical Analysis." *College Literature* 26: 162–95.

Kincheloe, Joe L., and George Staley. 1981. "Vietnam to Central America: A Case of Educational Failure." *USA Today*, July, 30–32.

Kincheloe, Joe L., and Shirley R. Steinberg. 1997. *Changing Multiculturalism*. Philadelphia: Open University Press.

————. 2000. "Constructing a Pedagogy of Whiteness for Angry White Students." In *Dismantling White Privilege: Pedagogy, Politics, and Whiteness*, edited by Nelson M. Rodriquez and Leila Vilaverde. New York: Peter Lang.

Kincheloe, Joe L., et al., eds. 1998. *White Reign: Deploying Whiteness in America*. New York: St. Martin's Press.

Kirk, H. David. 1964. *Shared Fate*. New York: Free Press.

Kirk, Russell. 1993. *America's British Culture*. New Brunswick, N.J.: Transaction Publishers.

Klumpp, James F. and T. A. Hollihan. 1979. "Debunking the Resignation of Earl Butz: Sacrificing an Official Racist." *Quarterly Journal of Speech* 65: 1–11.

Kovel, Joel. 1970. *White Racism: A Psychohistory*. New York: Vintage.

Kozol, J. 1991. *Savage Inequalities: Children in America's Schools*. (1st ed.). New York: Harper Perennial.

Kumashiro, K. K. 2001. "'Posts' Perspectives on Anti-oppressive Education in Social Studies, English, Mathematics, and Science Classrooms." *Educational Researcher* 30: 3–12.

Kumashiro, K. K. 2002. "Three Readings of D. Butin's Commentary" http://www.AERA/net. 31 (April).

Ladson-Billings, Gloria. 1996. "Silences as Weapons: Challenges of a Black Professor Teaching White Students." *Theory into Practice* 35: 79–85.

Laingen, Ambassador L. Bruce. 1992. *Yellow Ribbon: The Secret Journal of Bruce Laingen*. New York: Brassey's.

Langer, Suzanne K. 1984. *Mind: An Essay on Human Feeling*. Baltimore: Johns Hopkins University Press.

Lather, P. 1990. "Staying Dumb? Student Resistance to Liberatory Curriculum." Paper presented at the annual meeting of the American Educational Research Association, Boston.

Levin, B., et al. 1989. *Who Built America? Working People and the Nation's Economy, Politics and Culture*. New York: Pantheon Books.

Kimmel, Michael S., and Michael A. Messner, Eds. 2001. *Men's Lives*. 5th Ed. Boston: Allyn and Bacon.

Lorde, Audre. 1979. "The Great American Disease." *The Black Scholar* 10:16–20.

Lugg, Catherine A. 1996. *For God and Country: Conservatism and American School Policy*. New York: Peter Lang.

Lyman, Peter. 1981. "The Politics of Anger: On Silence, Ressentiment, and Political Speech." *Socialist Review* 57: 55–74.

Lynch, Frederick R. 1989. *Invisible Victims: White Males and the Crisis of Affirmative Action*. Westport, Conn.: Greenwood Press.

———. 1997. *The Diversity Machine: The Drive to Change the White Male Workplace*. New York: Free Press.

Marable, Manning. 1980. *From the Grassroots: Social and Political Essays toward Afro-American Liberation*. Boston: South End Press.

Mattingly, Carol. 2002. *Appropriate[ing] Dress: Women's Dress: Rhetorical Style in Nineteenth-Century America*. Carbondale: Southern Illinois University Press.

Mazurek, Raymond. 1999. "Freirian Pedagogy, Cultural Studies, and the Initiation of Students to Academic Discourse." In *Critical Literacy in Action: Writing Words, Changing Worlds*. New York: Boynton/Cook Heinemann: 208–322.

McCall, Ava L. 1994. "Rejoicing and Despairing: Dealing with Feminist Pedagogy in Teacher Education." *Teaching Education* 6: 59–69.

McGarry, Susan Hallsten. 1994. "Editor's Perspective." *Southwest Art*, July.

McIntosh, Peggy. 1993. "White Privilege: Unpacking the Invisible Knapsack." In *Experiencing Race, Class, and Gender in the United States*, edited by Virginia Cyrus. Mountain View: Calif.: Mayfield.

McIntyre, Alice. 1997. *Making Meaning of Whiteness: Exploring Racial Identity with White Teachers*. Albany: State University of New York Press.

McNamara, Robert. 1995. "The Final Briefing." *Pittsburgh Post-Gazette*, April 23: F1, 4.

McWilliams, Carey. 1948. *A Mask for Privilege: Anti-Semitism in America*. Boston: Little, Brown.

Melosh, Barbara. 1991. *Engendering Culture: Manhood and Womanhood in New Deal Public Art and Theater*. Washington, D.C.: Smithsonian Institution Press.

Mills, C. Wright. 1959. *The Sociological Imagination*. New York: Oxford University Press.

Modleski, T. 1991. *Feminism without Women: Culture and Criticism in a "Postfeminist" Age*. New York: Routledge.

Nash, Robert J. 1995. "A Neo-Essentialist Diatribe against American Education." *Journal of Teacher Education* 46: 150–55.

Nakayama, T. K., and R. L. Krizek. 1995. "Whiteness: A Strategic Rhetoric." *Quarterly Journal of Speech* 81: 291–309.

Nieburg, H. L. 1973. *Culture Storm: Politics and the Ritual Order*. New York: St. Martin's Press.

Nietzsche, Friedrich Wilhelm. 1966. *Beyond Good and Evil: Prelude to a Philosophy of the Future*. New York: Viking Press.

Norman, Elizabeth. 1990. *Women at War: The Story of Fifty Military Nurses Who Served in Vietnam*. Philadelphia: University of Pennsylvania Press.

Ottenhoff, John. 1994. "Of Wolves and Men." *Christian Century*, September, 859–61.

Parsons, Gerald. 1981. "Yellow Ribbons; Ties with Tradition." *Folklife Center News*, 4: 21, 9–12.

———. 1991. "How the Yellow Ribbon Became a National Folk Symbol. *Folklife Center News* 13(2): 9–11.

Phelan, Anne M. and H. James McLaughlin. 1995. "Educational Discourses, the Nature of the Child, and the Practice of New Teachers." *Journal of Teacher Education* 46: 165–74.

Phelan, P., and A. L. Davidson. 1994. "Looking across Borders: Students' Investigations of Family, Peer, and School Worlds as Cultural Therapy. In *Pathways to Cultural Awareness: Cultural Therapy with Teachers and Students*, edited by G. D. Spindler and L. Spindler. Thousand Oaks, Calif.: Corwin Press.

Pinderhughes, E. 1982. "Black Genealogy: Self-Liberator and Therapeutic Tool." *Smith College Studies in Social Work* 52: 93–106.

Powell, John A. 2000. "Whites Will Be Whites: The Failure to Interrogate Racial Privilege." *University of San Francisco Law Review* 34: 1–29.

Radaway, J. 1987. *Reading the Romance: Women, Patriarchy and Popular Literature*. London: Verso.

Rafferty, Max Lewis. 1970. *Classroom Countdown: Education at the Crossroads*. New York: Hawthorn Books.

Reagan, Ronald. 1984. Weekly Complication of Presidential Documents. U.S. Office of Federal Register, National Archives and Records Service, General Services Administration. Washington, D.C.: U.S. Government Printing Office.

Rich, Adrienne. 1979. *On Lies, Secrets, and Silence: Selected Prose, 1966–1978*. New York: Norton.

Rochlin, Gregory. 1973. *Man's Aggression: The Defense of the Self*. Boston: Gambit.

———. 1980. *The Masculine Dilemma: A Psychology of Masculinity*. Boston : Little, Brown.

Rodriguez, Fred. 1983. *Education in a Multicultural Society*. Washington, D.C.: University Press of America.

Rodriquez, Nelson M., and Leila Villaverde. 2000. *Dismantling White Privilege: Pedagogy, Politics, and Whiteness*. New York: Peter Lang.

Roediger, David 1991. *The Wages of Whiteness: Race and the Making of the American Working Class*. New York: Verso.

———. 1994. *Towards the Abolition of Whiteness.* New York: Verso.

Rosenberg, Pearl. 1997. "Underground Discourses: Exploring Whiteness in Teacher Education." In *Off White: Readings on Race, Power and Society,* edited by Michelle Fine et al. New York: Routledge.

Rosenberg, Tina. 1996. "Recovering from Apartheid." *New Yorker,* November 18: 86–95.

Roszak, Betty, and Theodore. 1969. *Masculine/Feminine Readings in Sexual Mythology and the Liberation of Women.* 1st ed. New York: Harper & Row.

Rothstein, Stanley William. 1994. *Schooling the Poor: A Social Inquiry into the American Educational Experience.* Westport, Conn: Bergin & Garvey.

Rudwick, E., and A. Meier. 1969. "Negro Retaliatory Violence in the Twentieth Century." In *The Making of Black America: Essays in Negro Life and History, vol. 2.* New York: Harper & Row.

Sagan, Eli. 1974. *Cannibalism: Human Aggression and Cultural Form.* New York: Harper & Row.

Salvio, P. 1994. "What Can a Body Know? Re-figuring Pedagogic Intention into Teacher Education." *Journal of Teacher Education* 20: 283–89.

Santino, Jack. 1992. "Yellow Ribbons and Seasonal Flags: The Folk Assemblage of War." *Journal of American Folklore* 105: 19–33.

Sartre, Jean-Paul. 1956. *The Anti-Semite and Jew.* New York: Washington Square Publishers.

Schacht, Steven P. 2000. "Using a Feminist Pedagogy as a Male Teacher: The Possibilities of a Partial and Situated Perspective." *Radical Pedagogy,* 2(2) http://radicalpedagogy.icaap.org.

Shor, Ira. 1996. *When Students Have Power: Negotiating Authority in a Critical Pedagogy.* Chicago : University of Chicago Press.

Shujaa, Mwalimu J., ed. 1996. *Beyond Segregation: The Politics of Quality in African American Schooling.* Thousand Oaks, Calif.: Corwin Press.

Simon, Roger I. 1991. *Learning Work: A Critical Pedagogy of Work Education.* New York: Bergin & Garvey.

———. 2001. *Divided We Stand: How Al Gore Beat George Bush and Lost the Presidency.* New York: Crown.

Siskel, Gene. 1994. "'Forrest Gump' Upholds a Great American Tradition." *Chicago Tribune,* July 8, 7, B4.

Sleeter, Christine E., and Peter L. McLaren, eds. 1995. *Multicultural Education, Critical Pedagogy, and the Politics of Difference.* Albany: State University of New York Press.

Slotkin, Richard. 1973. *Regeneration through Violence: The Mythology of the American Frontier, 1600–1860.* Middletown, Conn.: Wesleyan University Press.

Sowell, Thomas. 1994. *Inside American Education: Its Decline.* New York: Free Press.

Smolkin, Rachel. 2001. "Harvard Study Finds Large Divide in Northeast U.S. School." July 22. www.fairchance.org.

Spindler, G. D., and L. Spindler, eds. 1994. *Pathways to Cultural Awareness: Cultural Therapy with Teachers and Students.* Thousand Oaks, Calif.: Corwin Press.

Spring, Joel. 1995. *The Intersection of Cultures: Multicultural Education in the United States.* New York: McGraw-Hill.

Sykes, Heather. 1995. "Feminist Views on Radicals Pedagogies: Dangerous Struggles." *Journal of Teacher Education* 46: 71–73.

Taubin, Amy. 1994. "Two or Three Things: Plus Ça Change." *Village Voice*, August 9: 93.

Thompson, Audrey. 1999. Review of Off White: Readings on Race, Power and Society, edited by Michelle Fine et al. New York: Routledge. Online: http://www.ed.asu.edu/edrev/reviews/rev76.html.

Tizard, B., and A. Phoenix. 1993. *Black, White, or Mixed Race: Race and Racism in the Lives of Young People of Mixed Parentage*. New York: Routledge.

Travers, Peter. 1994. "Forrest Gump." *Rolling Stone*, July 14:99.

Tylee, Claire M. 1990. *The Great War and Women's Consciousness: Images of Militarism and Womanhood in Women's Writings, 1914–64*. Iowa City: University of Iowa Press.

Valades, Joseph, et al. 1997. "A Critical Case Study Approach to Questions of Identity and Racialized Mixed Heritage." *Journal of Critical Pedagogy* 1(1). Online: http://www.wmc.edu/academics/library/.

Valli, Linda. 1995. "The Dilemma of Race; Learning to Be Color Blind and Color Conscious." *Journal of Teacher Education* 46: 120–29.

Van Biema, David. 1994. "Forrest Gump Is Dumb." *Time*, August 24: 82.

Waller, James. 1998. *Face to Face: The Changing State of Racism across America*. New York: Plenum Press.

Weiner, Lois. 1993. *Preparing Teachers for Urban Schools: Lessons from Thirty Years of School Reform*. New York: Teachers College Press.

Weis, Lois. 1995. "Constructing the 'Other': Discursive Renditions of White Working-Class Males in High School." In *Critical Theory and Educational Research*, edited by Peter L. McLaren and James M. Giarelli. Albany: SUNY Press: 203–22.

Weis, L., et al. 1997. "Re-examining 'A Moment in History': Loss of Privilege inside White, Working-Class Masculinity in the 1990's." In *Off White: Readings on Society, Race and Culture*, edited by Michelle Fine et al. New York: Routledge.

Werbner, Richard P. 1989. *Ritual Passage, Sacred Journey: The Process and Organization of Religious Movement*. Washington, D.C.: Smithsonian Institution Press.

Wertsch, J. V. 1985. *Vygotsky and the Social Formation of Mind*. Cambridge, Mass.: Harvard University Press.

White, Louise R. 1973. "Effective Teachers for Inner City Schools." *Journal of Negro Education* 42: 308–14.

Wilden, Anthony. 1988. *System and Structure: Essays in Communication and Exchange*, 2d ed. London: Tavistock.

Williamson, Bruce. 1994. "Forrest Gump," *Playboy*, September 4, 26.

Wilson, William Julius. 1980. *The Declining Significance of Race: Blacks and Changing American Institutions*, 2d ed. Chicago: University of Chicago Press.

Winant, Howard. 1997. "Behind Blue Eyes: Whiteness and Contemporary U.S. Racial Politics." In *Off White: Readings on Race, Power and Society*, edited by Michelle Fine et al. New York: Routledge. Online: http://www.blue.temple.edu/~winant/whiteness.html.

Wortham, Stanton. 1994. *Acting Out Participant Examples in the Classroom*. Philadelphia: J. Benjamins.

———. 2001. *Narratives in Action: A Strategy for Research and Action*. New York: Teachers College Press.

Wu, William F. 1982. *Chinese Americans in American Fiction, 1850–1940*. Hamden, Conn.: Archon Books.

Yeo, Frederick L. 1997a. *Inner-City Schools, Multiculturalism, and Teacher Education: A Professional Journey.* New York: Garland Press.

———. 1997b. "Teacher Preparation and Inner City Schools: Sustaining Educational Failure." *Urban Review* 29: 127–43.

Zimmerman, Jonathan. 2002. *Whose America?: Culture Wars in the Public Schools.* Cambridge, Mass.: Harvard University Press.

INDEX

Studies in the Postmodern Theory of Education

General Editors
Joe L. Kincheloe & Shirley R. Steinberg

Counterpoints publishes the most compelling and imaginative books being written in education today. Grounded on the theoretical advances in criticalism, feminism, and postmodernism in the last two decades of the twentieth century, Counterpoints engages the meaning of these innovations in various forms of educational expression. Committed to the proposition that theoretical literature should be accessible to a variety of audiences, the series insists that its authors avoid esoteric and jargonistic languages that transform educational scholarship into an elite discourse for the initiated. Scholarly work matters only to the degree it affects consciousness and practice at multiple sites. Counterpoints' editorial policy is based on these principles and the ability of scholars to break new ground, to open new conversations, to go where educators have never gone before.

For additional information about this series or for the submission of manuscripts, please contact:

> Joe L. Kincheloe & Shirley R. Steinberg
> c/o Peter Lang Publishing, Inc.
> 275 Seventh Avenue, 28th floor
> New York, New York 10001

To order other books in this series, please contact our Customer Service Department:

> (800) 770-LANG (within the U.S.)
> (212) 647-7706 (outside the U.S.)
> (212) 647-7707 FAX

Or browse online by series:

> www.peterlangusa.com